TAUNTON FLOWER S

The Oldest Longest Running Show in the Country

Aerial View of the Flower Show in Vivary Park 2012.

The moral right of Anne Leamon to be identified as the author of this work has been asserted by her in accordance with the Copyright, Designs and Patents Act 1988.

Copyright © Anne Leamon 2013

All rights reserved. No part of this publication may be reproduced, stored in a retrieval system or transmitted in any form or by any means, electronic, mechanical, photocopying, recording or otherwise, without the prior permission of both the copyright owner and the publisher of this book.

ISBN 978-0-9576520

Published by Anne Leamon

Preface

I first became aware of Taunton Flower Show when, as a child, my mother used to take me on the pillion of her bicycle to the Show mainly to see the Competitive entries. She was President of the local Women's Institute and they always entered the Carter Cup Class for Women's Institutes. Mum always hoped to win but her Women's Institute was sadly unlucky, usually coming second or third!

I remember vividly, however, being taken by my brothers one late afternoon to the Fun Fair in Wilton Lands. The wonder of the colour and noise, the Noah's Ark, and the dodgems, never before seen. And of course, the fireworks, often viewed from the top of Blagdon Hill on a clear night – magical!

When I was older I used to go on my own after school to the Flower Show – not really to see the plants but to see the outside stands, especially the Army one as I wanted to join the Army when older. The year they brought their parachute tower was especially memorable. The nervous anticipation of climbing the tower, viewing the show site from above, but then the thrill of jumping off, to float gently down to earth.

For several years later I had an outside stand selling fuchsias, pelargoniums and other plants produced on my nursery but then I was invited to mount a display in the Trade Tent, as it was then. I had made the grade! It was amazing competing against Otter Nurseries, Scotts Nurseries or Cadbury Garden Centre, all of us sadly no longer exhibiting and to hear the comments of the public as they wandered past the stand.

And so here follows a brief history of the Taunton Horticultural and Floricultural Society. I trust you will enjoy reading it, and you will feel as I do that Taunton Flower Show is still among the best Flower Shows in the country as it has been hailed throughout it's long history from 1831 to the present day. I am indebted to my husband for researching all the newspaper reports from 1831 which is how I have managed to find out so much about the Society.

Should you have any memorabilia of the Shows you would like to share please contact me.

Anne Leamon
Vice President
Taunton Horticultural and Floricultural Society
July 2013

1831-1850 The early years

Taunton Flower Show held it's first show in September **1831** and took place in the Assembly Rooms on the Parade, Taunton. Subsequent shows were held in other venues including the new Market Hall, (on the Parade) and the Winchester Arms on Castle Green, before moving to Vivary Park, owned by Mr. Kinglake, in 1851 where it has continued to flourish. This makes this the oldest, longest running Flower Show in the Country.

The Market House on the centre of the Parade, Taunton, was built in 1772 on a site that had previously been cleared of houses. This picture shows the Market Hall arcades viewed from East Street.

The Parade provided a focal point for the centre of the town and it was here that a twice weekly market was held until 1929.

The Assembly rooms were on the first floor.

The Arcades were removed in 1930 and a small area remains facing Corporation Street but the rest of the area is now paved over.

The aim of the Society was *'the encouragement of horticulture in its various branches, by means of premiums to be given for the best specimens of flowers, fruit and vegetables'.* These aims are still being achieved 181 years later.

From the start however, it was the gentlemen who won the prizes depending upon how good their gardeners were - in 1831, Fruit Classes - Pine Apples 1st Prize Sir T. B. Lethbridge, Bart of Sandhill Park, Bishops Lydeard, gardener E. Stanley, and Black Grapes – 1st Prize Thomas Clifton Esq. of Hatch Court, Hatch Beauchamp, W. Kelway gardener. Bear in mind that gentlefolk lived in large houses with gardens which provided most of their flowers, fruit and vegetables and gardeners were highly prized, being paid as much as 10s. 0d a week in 1831 – but not when it came to acknowledging them in competitions, it was the owners who received the prizes not the workers!

Gentlemen exhibitors came from all over the country and included the Marquis of Bath, the Earl of Cork, the Earl of Radnor, the Duke of Wellington, Sir Henry Hoare of Stourhead, Lady Smyth of Ashton Court, Mr. Luttrell of Dunster Castle, Lord Wharton, and The Marchioness Curzon of Kedleston Hall, Derbyshire.

The show, now known locally as the Chelsea of the West, has always been judged to be of great importance with many new plant varieties being introduced to the public. Trade exhibits have come from all over the country and the show has become internationally known with exhibits from Canada, Holland, Japan, New Zealand and the United States of America.

Ataccia (Tacca) Cristata introduced by Jack 1821.

Dendrobium fimbriatum introduced by Veitch 1830's.

Nurserymen exhibiting at the Show have included James Veitch of Killerton, whose family later sponsored plant hunters and introduced many new plants to this country; Kelways of Langport responsible for introductions of peonies and gladiolus; Blackmore and Langdon, producing new delphiniums and begonias; James Cypher of Cheltenham who specialised in growing and exporting exotics all over the world; Luccombe Pince and Co. Exeter who introduced the Luccombe Oak, Quecus x hispanica.

The British Gladioli, Carnation, National Dahlia, and Rose Societies have all held their national and international shows at Taunton Flower Show.

Taunton Vale was, and still is, a very fertile area for growing plants, flowers and vegetables. Situated between the Blackdown Hills on the South, the Quantocks to the North, the Brendons to the West and the Poldens to the East it is the land of the summer or 'Zummerset' as it is known to the locals.

A report in the Taunton Courier of the 6th July 1831 stated:-
'that it is in contemplation to establish a Horticultural Society for the vale of Taunton, to be supported by small annual contributions, which shall have for its object, the encouragement of horticulture in its various branches, by means of premiums to be given for the best specimens of flowers, fruit and vegetables, to be exhibited at meetings held for the purpose'.

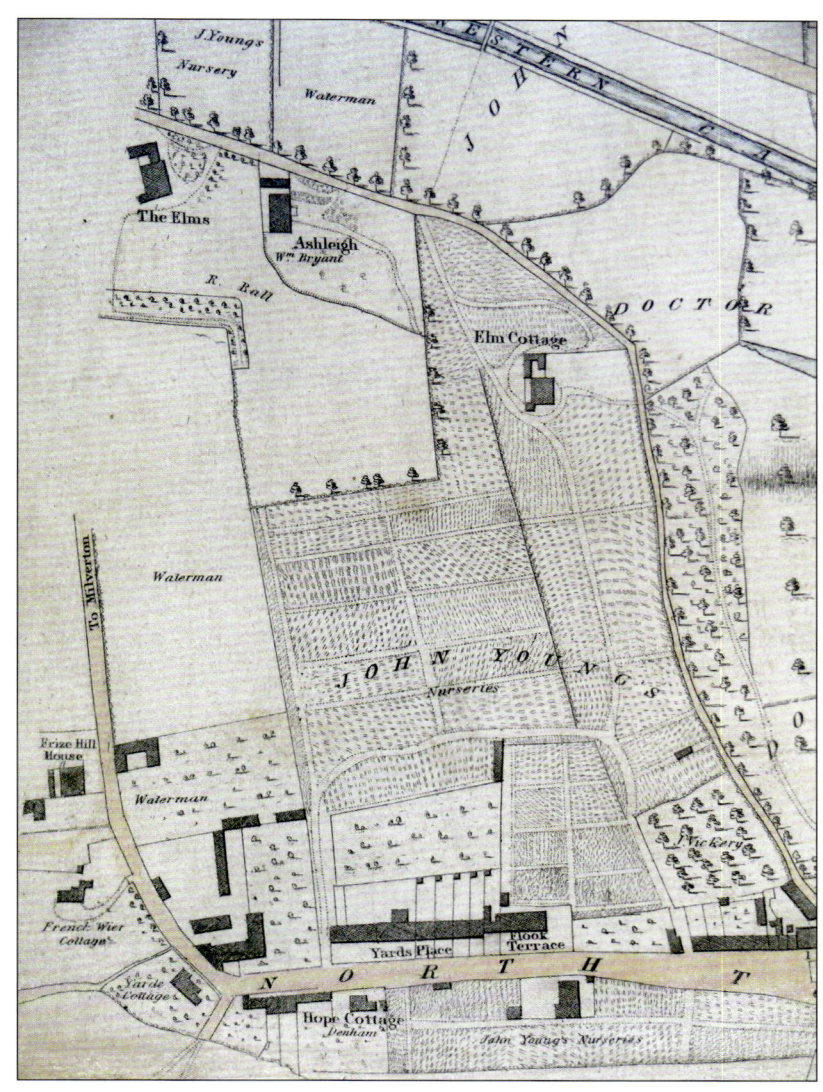

John Young's extensive nursery in the Staplegrove area from Wood's 1840 map of Taunton.

The Elms shown on the above map.

Mr. E. M. Sandford (1794-1871) who lived at Nynehead Court, was a JP and represented both Taunton and later Minehead in Parliament, and became Deputy Lieutenant of the County, agreed to be President. A public meeting was held on Wednesday 3rd August 1831 at the Market House, Taunton where Mr. F. Popham Esq. who lived at Bagborough House, Bishops Lydeard, was appointed Chairman. The various rules and regulations were decided, a liberal subscription was agreed and it was announced that the first exhibition should take place in September, 1831. Mr. J. Young of Young's Nursery, Staplegrove, Taunton who had instigated the Society, agreed to be Secretary.

Shows were originally held in the afternoons, gates opening to the subscribers at 1.30 p.m. public being admitted later and the show closing by 6 p.m. The subscribers were mainly the local gentry who paid a subscription of one guinea in 1836 (in 1866 subscribers tickets cost half a guinea which admitted three people up to three o'clock). This enabled them to enter the competitions for which their gardeners prepared the exhibits. When prizes were awarded the gardener's name was put in brackets after the name of the gentleman/woman winning the prize. In 1832, three shows were held, in 1833 and 1834, four shows were held, 1835, three shows and then 1836 and 1837 two shows were held with one show in 1844. The shows took place in May, August and September, and the plants exhibited represented spring, summer and autumn respectively.

> **TAUNTON AND WEST SOMERSET HORTICULTURAL SOCIETY,**
>
> THE FIRST EXHIBITION of this SOCIETY will be held at the MARKET HOUSE, TAUNTON, on FRIDAY, the 16th of SEPTEMBER next, when Prizes are offered for the following Articles:—
>
> Pine Apples, Grapes, Peaches, Nectarines, Apricots, Plums, Damsons, Pears, Apples, Mulberries, Figs, Quinces, Filberts, Nuts, Gooseberries, Currants, Cauliflowers, Brocoli, Celery, Carrots, Parsnips, Onions, Peas, Cucumbers, Dahlias, Stove Plants, Greenhouse Plants, Hardy Annuals, Tender Annuals, Hardy Perennials, Hardy Shrubs.
>
> COTTAGERS' PRIZES. Vegetables of any sort, Fruits, do. Flowers do. Honey.
>
> The Committee particularly request that every Article to be exhibited for a Prize may be in the Room by 10 o'clock in the forenoon, on the day of exhibition, and they respectfully solicit contributions of Flowers and Plants for decorating the room.
>
> Tickets of admission may be had at the door, or by applying to Mr. JOHN YOUNG, Nurseryman, Taunton, of whom may also be obtained, gratis, printed particulars of the articles to be exhibited. Dated August 15, 1831.

On 17th August 1831 this advertisement appeared in the Taunton Courier. Although the Show was due to be held on 16th September, because of the increased heat of the weather which had ripened the wall fruit and other garden crops earlier than normal, the Exhibition date was brought forward to 9th September 1831.

1831 – 9th September 2 p.m. The first Taunton Flower Show was held in the Assembly Rooms on the first floor of the Market House (now the Parade Rooms) on the Parade, Taunton. The room, which was 50ft x 30ft x 24ft high, was spectacularly decorated with a star of Dahlias of almost every possible diversity of colour from Young's Nursery, another star and a crown of dahlias by Mr. Veitch, of Killerton, two finely covered hop-poles provided by Mr. Ham of Orchard Portman; Messrs Dymond and Messrs Luccombe of Exeter displayed baskets of admirable specimens of dahlias. Arranged around the room were a variety of fruits, flowers and vegetables for competition, so many entries that the prize giving took a considerable time. The classes were for the gardeners of the gentry and consisted of 11 fruit, 8 vegetable, and 17 flower including 8 classes of dahlias. The nurserymen classes consisted of two fruit and 17 flower. The Cottagers' competition consisted of four classes - fruit, vegetables, flowers (any sort) and honey. The novelty of the occasion brought about a considerable influx of fashionable company to the town, and at one time the room was completely filled by spectators.

> TAUNTON AND WEST SOMERSET HORTICULTURAL SOCIETY.—The First Exhibition of this Society was held at the Assembly Rooms on Friday week. The number of persons present on this interesting occasion amounted to about four hundred, and consisted of all the beauty and fashion of the town and neighbourhood. The following list of prizes, and of those who obtained them, will shew the variety & interest of the exhibition:
>
> FRUITS.—*Pine Apples*: the first prize was awarded to E. Stanley, gardener to Sir T. B. Lethbridge, bart. Sandhill Park; the 2d prize to J. Hay, gardener to E. A. Sanford, esq; M.P. of Nynehead Court.—*Melons*: first prize to John Gamlin, gardener to the Rev. A. Foster, of Kingston; 2d prize to Wm. Jennings, gardener to Francis Popham, esq; of Bagborough House.—*Black Grapes*: 1st prize to Wm. Kelway, gardener to Thos. Clifton, esq; of Hatch Court. *White Grapes*: the same.—*Peaches*: 1st prize to James Quaint, gardener to the Rev. W. P. Thomas, of Wellington; 2d prize to E. Stanley, gardener to Sir T. B. Lethbridge, bart.—*Nectarines*: 1st prize to James Reed, gardener to J. A. Martin, esq; of West Monkton; 2d prize to the Rev. J. R. Fenwick.—*Plums*: 1st prize to Jas. Reed; 2d to J. Hay.—*Damsons*: to Wm. Kelway.—*Pears*: 1st prize to Jas. Reed; 2d to Chas. Holcombe Dare, esq; of North Curry.—*Apples*: 1st prize to Jas. Reed; 2d to J. Akers, gardener to Edward J. Esdaile, esq; of Cotheleston; 3d to Wm. Kelway.—*Strawberries*: to W. Jennings, gardener to F. Popham, esq.
>
> ROOTS.—*Parsnips*: to Henry Warre, esq; of Bishop's Lydeard.—*Carrots*: to Wm. Kingdon, gardener to the Rev. W. Wood, of Staplegrove.—*Onions*: 2d prize to Wm. Kelway.—*Beet*, Poiree a carte blanche, extra prize, to R. Reed, gardener to Mrs. Walrond.
>
> VEGETABLES.—*Cucumbers*: 1st prize to John Lindley, gardener to Mrs. Hawker; 2d to H. Samson, gardener to the Rev. E. J. Halliday, of Yard House.—*Celery*: to J. Quaint, gardener to the Rev. W. P. Thomas.—*Peas*: 1st prize to the Rev. J. R. Fenwick; 2d to John Lindley.—*Beans*: to the Rev. J. R. Fenwick.—*Capsicums*: to Wm. Kingdon.
>
> FLOWERS.—*Dahlias*: Crimson or Moreen, 1st prize to Wm. Jennings, gardener to Francis Popham, esq.; 2d to Mrs. Speke. Scarlet: 1st prize to Mrs. Speke; 2d to Wm. Jennings. Purple: 1st prize to ditto; 2d to Mrs. Speke. Lilac: 1st prize to Wm. Gamlin; 2d to Mrs. Speke. Light Shades: 1st to ditto; 2d to G. H. Carew, esq.—*Seedling Dahlias*: to John Lindley. *Globe ditto*: 1st prize to ditto; 2d to John Hammond, gardener to Fred. Grey Cooper, esq; of Barton Grange.—*Stove Plants*: 1st prize to H. Sansom, gardener to the Rev. E. J. Halliday. *Tender Exotic*, Ditto.—*Green-House Plants*: 1st to J. Gamlin; 2d to Mrs. Cliffe, of Wilton. *Tender Exotic*, to J. Gamlin.—*Tender Exotic*: extra prize, to Mrs. Vanzandt, of Netherclay House, Bishop's Hull.—*Bouquet of Hardy Annuals*, to John Lindley; *Ditto of Tender Annuals*, to J. Hatherley, gardener to R. F. Beauchamp, esq; of Walford House.—*Hardy Shrub*: to Mrs. Cliffe.—*Tall Crimson Cockscombs*: extra prize, to R. Reed.

A newspaper report of the first Taunton Flower Show, September 1831.

Nurserymen came great distances to exhibit their plants – amongst them Mr. Veitch of Killerton, founder of Veitch's Nurseries of Exeter, whose descendants financed plant hunters; Messrs Luccombe and Co. and Dymond and Co. both nurserymen from Exeter. These, coupled with Mr. John Young of Staplegrove Nurseries and Hammond and Stevens, both of Taunton, mounted an excellent show of dahlias, greenhouse plants, hollyhocks, hardy annuals and hardy perennials at the first show and continued to support the show for several years.

Lets' imagine just for a moment, the roads around Taunton. They were mainly of mud and stones, with many pot holes, especially when wet. These were the main roads – side roads could well have been very rutted and consisted mainly of mud. Transport was either by horseback, coaches or wagons pulled by horses, and shanks' pony. No bicycles, the bone shaker was invented in 1865, made entirely of wood with metal tyres. There was a train line running from Bristol to Exeter but this by-passed Taunton. Taunton station was opened in July 1842. John Macadam's invention of rolling a hard layer of stones into the soil and covering it with gravel, which would be ground into powder by the iron-rimmed wheels of the traffic was not in use until 1856. This would probably have been used for the road from Exeter to Taunton then and allowed traffic to travel at a maximum speed of 12 miles per hour.

The exhibits had to be in place at the Show for the judging before the expected 1.30 p.m. opening to the visitors.

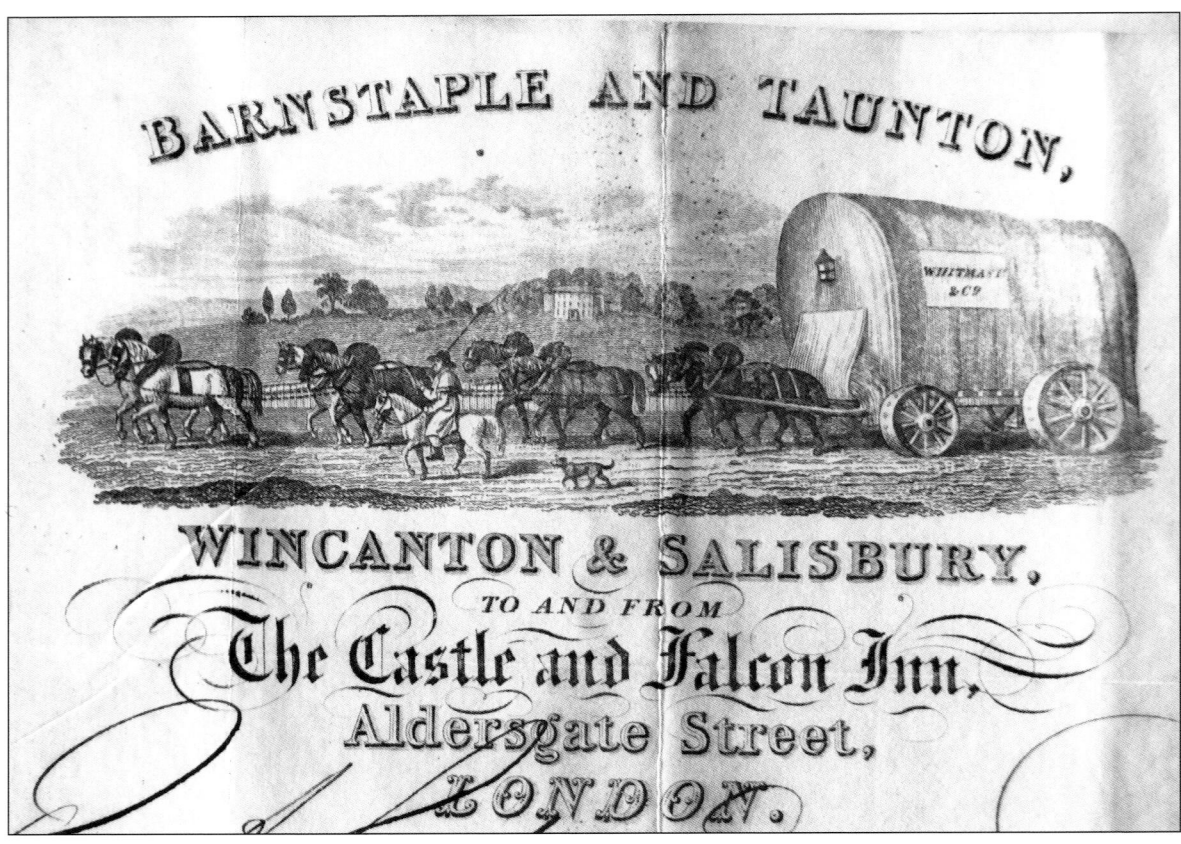

Horses and wagon which could have been used for transporting plants to the Flower Show from afar.

Every plant, fruit and vegetable that was exhibited at the Taunton Flower Shows from 1831-1851 had to be transported by horse and cart, whether it came from the surrounding area of Taunton or as far away as Exeter.

This obviously caused difficulties, trying to ensure that the exhibits arrived at the Show in pristine condition so a Flower Stand and Show case could have been used to transport the flowers.

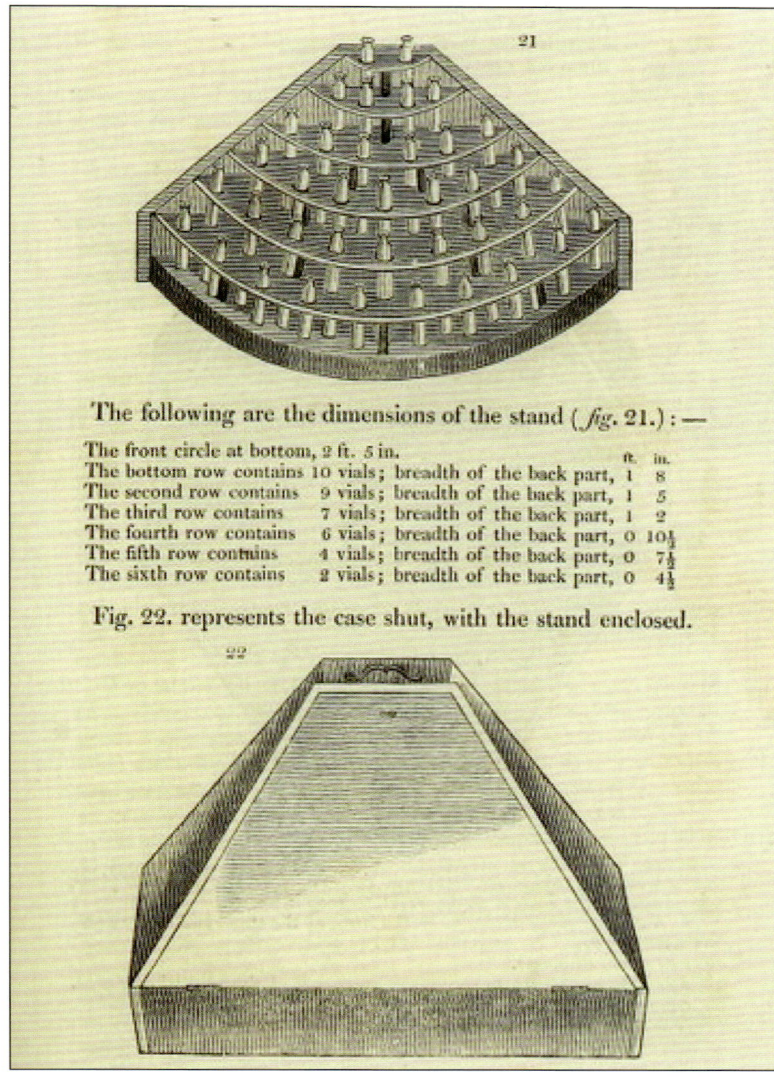

A Flower Stand and Show Case

A sketch of a flower stand and case used for conveying specimens of roses, pinks, dahlias and other flowers from place to place without injury.

Every flower is placed in a phial of water, each of which shows only its top above the shelf on which it appears and the flower stem, passing through the next shelf below, rests upon that phial under, which keeps them all steady. Those of the lower row are shorter.

The great convenience of this stand is that it makes a pretty appearance, when filled with flowers and two of them placed back to back form an elegant display.

At the first Annual Meeting in January 1832 the following comments were made:-

"The numerous and very respectable attendance testified the interest which was felt in the objects of the Society and so far as your Committee can form a judgment, the interests of Horticulture in this district, are likely to be promoted by it. To one object in particular your Committee would earnestly direct your attention, viz. the encouragement of Cottage Horticulture by the offering of premiums to illustrious cottagers, for the products of their gardens, whether fruits, flowers, vegetables or honey".

The report went on to suggest that: *"the Committee took the liberty of recommending those gentlemen who have opportunities to endeavour to convince their poorer neighbours, who have gardens, of the advantages of keeping bees: and for any honey exhibited by this class of persons, they would recommend liberal prizes being given"* and finished with *"you would have the satisfaction of knowing you have been the means of inducing any of your cottage neighbours to spend an hour in the cultivation of their gardens, which might otherwise have been wasted at the public house"*!

Andromeda polifolia (Bog Rosemary).

Serpent Cucumbers.

John Young of Young's Nurseries, Staplegrove, Secretary of the first shows, exhibited this heath plant from the Turf Moor near Bridgwater at the first show of the year in May 1832.

Kidney beans, cucumbers, lemons and sweet water grapes were also amongst the exhibits.

Two more shows were held in 1832. In June, cherries, strawberries, melons and grapes were amongst the exhibits, and in September, a Serpent Cucumber nearly three feet long caused much comment. There were 16 fruit classes, 2 nut classes, 6 flower classes, 12 vegetable classes, honey classes and for the cottagers, fruit, vegetable and honey classes.

In **May 1833**, in the Assembly Rooms, Double Dutch Anemones, a new plant introduction, were shown by Messrs. Luccombe, Pince & Co. of Exeter. This was the first season of their flowering in England; they consisted of 101 distinctly named varieties, and certainly surpassed in size, colour and brilliance everything hitherto produced in this way. Mr. Young exhibited specimens of the new herbaceous Calceolarias which interested the spectators.

Three more shows were held in **1833**, in June and August in the Assembly Rooms and October at the Market House.

At the October Show of 1833, the prizes for fruit, flowers and vegetables included 56 prizes for dessert apples, 26 prizes for dessert pears, 39 prizes for Georginas or Dahlias and 21 prizes for seedling Georginas or Dahlias. The apples and pears were classed as follows: Apples, Pippins of sorts, Nonpareils, Pearmains, Reinettes, Codlins and Russets. The Committee also requested that no mark of a cross or seal should be used as private marks for the several articles exhibited.

At the May show in **1834** the classes were now advertised as Gentlemen's Plants and Flowers, Gentlemen's Fruits and Vegetables, Nurserymen's Plants and Flowers and Cottagers' and included Cucumbers, Potatoes – forced, Asparagus, Mushrooms and Sea Kale. At the August show, held in the New Market, Cottagers entering the competition, required a note from a subscriber recommending him, certifying that the articles were 'bona fide' of his own growth, otherwise his entry would not be admitted!

TAUNTON AND WEST SOMERSET HORTICULTURAL SOCIETY.

THE THIRD EXHIBITION of this Society for the present Year, will be held on TUESDAY, the 26th August, when Prizes are offered for the following Articles:—

Pine Apples	Hardy Perennials
Grapes	Indica Odorata and Noisette Roses
Apples	
Peaches	Hardy Annuals
Nectarines	China Asters
Apricots	Cockscombs
Plums	Balsams
Pears	Georginas or Dahlias
Melons	Celery
Cherries	Carrots
Figs	Onions
Strawberries	Beet
Gooseberries	Autumnal Brocoli
Currants	Capsicums
Stove plants	Green Peas.
Greenhouse ditto	Honey

Articles of Superior Merit not specified above.

COTTAGERS'.

Apples	Onions
Fruit of any other kind	Scarlet Runners
Turnips	Nosegay
Potatoes	Honey
Carrots	

JOHN YOUNG, Hon. Sec.

Dated August 2, 1834.

N.B. Every Cottager desirous of exhibiting any Articles for a Prize, must bring a note from the Subscriber recommending him, certifying that the articles are, *bona fide*, his own growth, or he will not be allowed to compete.

The gate admission amounted to £15.00. New classes included Figs, Mulberries, Currants, and Red Celery. The Cottager's classes included named vegetables, honey and a Nosegay (posy).

By **1835** the Shows were becoming so popular that subscribers tickets were lodged at the banks of Messrs Stuckey & Co. and Messrs Badcock and they could collect these on payment of their subscription. Non subscribers' tickets, to be bought in advance, cost 2s 6d, (£6.50 in present day) for admission at 2 o'clock and 1s.(£2.50) for admission at 3 o'clock, to be bought from Miss Fearncombe's, Fore Street or the Secretary.

As can be seen, with wages for the working man at approximately 5s (£12.50) a week, admission to the show was more for the gentry than the working classes. Nobody was to be admitted without a ticket and no plants would be received after 10 o'clock.

After each Show, plants had normally been sold off to the public but at the last Show of 1835 in September, held back in the Assembly rooms, this practice was discontinued so that the room could be cleared at an early hour.

Epacris Tauntoniensis

This free flowering hybrid was raised by Mr. Ball, Nurseryman of Taunton, who took over Mr. Young's nursery at Staplegrove. This plant was a cross between Epacris grandiflora and Epacris impressa. Flowering on the nursery in December 1847 in a greenhouse, this plant could be planted outside during the summer but was brought into the greenhouse before the winter to avoid being damaged by frost.

Two of the classes in the May 1835 show were for asparagus, not less than 50 spears and French beans not less than 100 beans. Although there were Cottagers classes for fruit, flowers, vegetables and honey at each of the three shows in 1835, the only prizes awarded in May and July were for Nosegays (posies). Presumably for some reason no cottager had entered the other classes but in the September show cottagers won prizes for honey, onions, Nosegays, apples, dahlias, French beans and filberts. There were, however, numerous entries at each show from both the gentry and nurserymen.

A huge pumpkin which weighed 98 pounds and measured five feet six inches in circumference was exhibited by the Rev. Cecil Smith of Bishops Lydeard in 1836.

Pine apple as exhibited in 1834 at Taunton Flower Show.

Peach Princess of Wales.

In April **1836** a short advert alerted ladies and gentlemen to the fact that the Society was in decline and advertised the holding of a meeting at Sweet's Hotel, Castle Green, Taunton, to determine whether the Society could continue. The Subscription for the Year was set at One Guinea (£52.00) and for Nurserymen and Public Gardeners 10s. (£25.00). The admittance fee to the public was reduced to 1s. (£2.50) An exhibition (show) took place 10th June 1836, held in the Assembly Rooms of the Market House on the Parade.

It is interesting that a note is made that peas and potatoes were not to be forced! Comment was also made that every article exhibited should be the *bona fide* property of the exhibitor and have been in his possession six months previous to the time of Exhibition. One can only draw the conclusion that doubt had been raised as to the validity of some of the exhibits people were entering!

However, the Society once again flourished with a delightful exhibition of flowers and fruits at the June show and it was felt that it would continue prosperously in the future. After the September show a dinner, tickets 3s 6d, was held in Sweets Hotel for some 40 ladies and gentlemen (the prize fruit being served as dessert).

It was suggested that a meeting be held in Bridgwater, alternately with Taunton, to increase the prosperity of the Society.

In May **1837** Messrs Hammond and Stevens, Castle Green Nursery, Taunton, exhibited the most striking exhibit in the room – Calceolaria Splendida raised by them in 1836. The remarkable plant had on it nearly 200 flowers – it was to be sent off that day, after the show, to London and exhibited in Messrs Flanagan and Nutting's shop, Mansion House Street, London. Hammond and Stevens also exhibited a Tropaelum Tricolorum - the plant measured ten feet high by four feet wide.

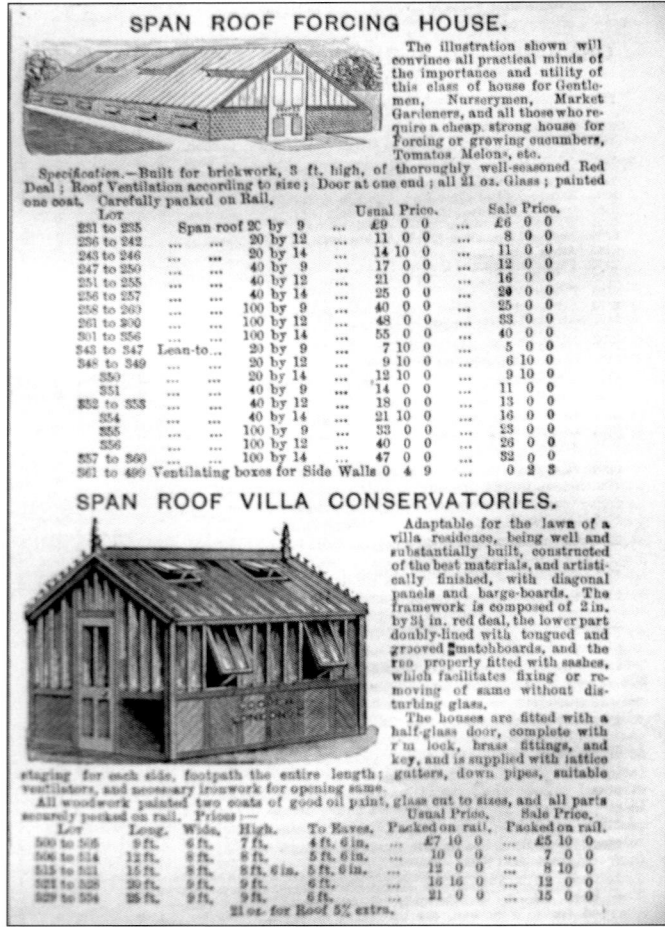

An advert for forcing houses and conservatories available to nurserymen, market gardeners and the gentry. The houses would have been heated by hot water pipes running around the inside of the building alongside the brick walls. Shelving erected above provided an area for forcing plants in pots. These houses were also used to grow pine apples, peaches, nectarines, cucumbers, melons and tomatoes.

Some gardeners used horse manure mixed with straw in deep beds in greenhouses and frames to provide heat to bring on crops earlier than normal.

Cottage gardeners used urine and sewage from the house. It was buried in the garden and the area left for a time until the pathogens had died a natural death and the soil became extremely fertile.

In **1837** the following reports occurred in the Somerset County Gazette and Western Flying Post referring to the May and September shows.

Taunton and West Somerset Horticultural Society. — May 19. This was the first meeting of this society. The company was respectable, but not numerous. There was a very fine show of plants. Amongst the gentlemen's gardeners, Mr. Duncan, the excellent and scientific gardener to R. F. Beauchamp, Esq., gained, and deservedly, the greatest number of prizes. Amongst the nurserymen, by far the greatest number of prizes were awarded to Messrs. Hammond and Stephens. The most striking specimen in the room was their Calceolària splèndida, raised by them last year. This remarkable plant had on it nearly 200 flowers, and was universally admitted to be the finest that has been shown in Taunton. It was sent off to London immediately after the show, to be exhibited in Messrs. Flannagan and Nutting's shop, Mansion-House Street. Messrs. Hammond and Stephens also exhibited two very large plants of Tropæ'olum tricolòrum, one of which measured 10 ft. in height and 4 ft. in width. Mr. Veitch had also a beautiful small plant of the same, but more fully in flower, which was truly splendid. The show was also much indebted to Mr. Veitch for many other new and beautiful creeping plants. Mr. Young obtained a prize for a fine collection of heaths, which were much admired and formed one of the most interesting objects in the room. (*Somerset County Gazette*, May 20.)

Sept. 22. Among the prizes were for nurserymen, Hammond and Stevens, dahlias, bouquet of; collection of; seedling dahlias; hardy annuals; each the first prize. John Young, ericas, extra prize; green-house plants, roses, ornamental basket of cut flowers; ditto of hardy plants; bouquet of dahlias; star of dahlias; each the first prize. Webber and Pierce, dahlias, awarded the first prize; but afterwards withdrawn, in consequence of their being brought after time. (*Western Flying Post*, Oct. 2. 1837.)

*Epacris grandiflora 1825
(Fuchsia Heath).*

*Kennedia nigricans
John Lindley 1835.*

Mention was made of the superb plants sent by Sir F. Cooper, Bart. Barton Grange, Corfe, such as Kennedia nigricans, great credit being paid to Mr. Hunt, the gardener. From the gardens of R. F. Beauchamp Esq. of Tetton House, Kingston St. Mary, came some fine specimens of stove and green-house plants such as Epacris grandiflora, seven feet high, and most splendidly in bloom (Australian Fuchsia Heath) first recorded in cultivation in England in 1825.

*Rose Devoniensis, introduced in 1838, by Mr. Foster of Devonshire.
Best grown in a greenhouse or warm southern climate, the
finest of its kind was exhibited by Mr. H. P. Collins of Hatch Park, near Taunton.*

Advert for Robert Poynter Seedsman & Nurseryman who had a nursery at Castle Green and nursery grounds at Staplegrove. The nursery was in existence in 1822 run by Richard Bacon and continued under Henry Hammond and Thomas Stephens. Robert Poynter took over the nursery in 1859 and he retired in 1900.

There follows a gap until September **1840** when a show was staged at the Winchester Arms, Castle Green, Taunton and was well supported by the local gentry such as Lady Cooper, of Barton House, Corfe. The dahlias were the best varieties ever seen at Taunton and there was also a very fine collection of Heart's Ease, Cockscombs, Fuchia Fulgens and many other articles of great merit. Once again, after the show the subscribers sat down to an excellent dinner prepared by Mrs. Foy.

The nurserymen of the area exhibited a beautiful collection of dahlias, but did not compete for prizes.

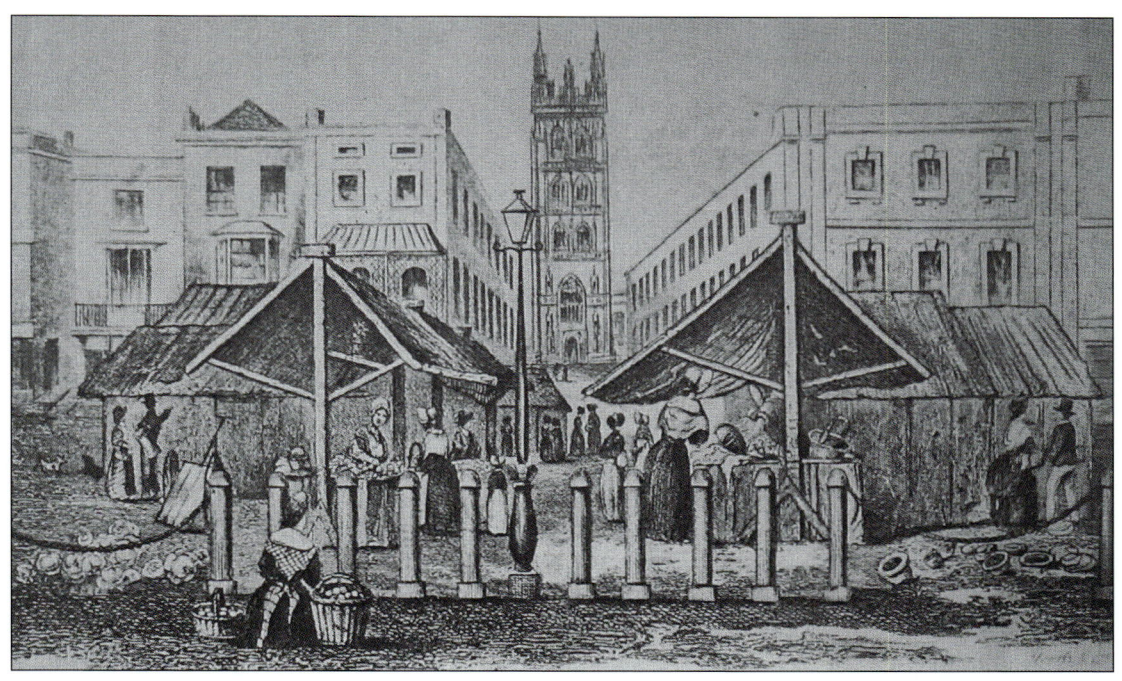

The Parade, Taunton, with Market Stalls about 1845.

Again another gap until **1844** when a note appeared in the Taunton Courier stating *'That the horticultural exhibitions in this town, which for several years past have been discontinued, are to be renewed under the auspices of several respectable gentlemen, who have kindly consented to co-operate with professional floriculturists for that purpose'.* Unfortunately no show reports have been found to support this statement.

But in October, **1850** it was announced that ***"Messrs Horsey and Penny have kindly undertaken to act as Provincial Secretaries and a meeting of the Amateur Florists of this town and neighbourhood will shortly be called"***

Mendinilla magnifica introduced by Veitch 1850.

Hexacentris mysorensis introduced by Wight 1845.

1851-1945 Another beginning – first time in Vivary Park

In June 1851 the show moved to Vivary Park and was staged at the High Street end of the Park, courtesy of Mr. Kinglake who owned the Park.

View of the Park entrance from the top of High Street.

*Clianthus dampieri
Introduced by Veitch 1850.*

*Clematis lanuginose
Introduced by Lindley 1850's.*

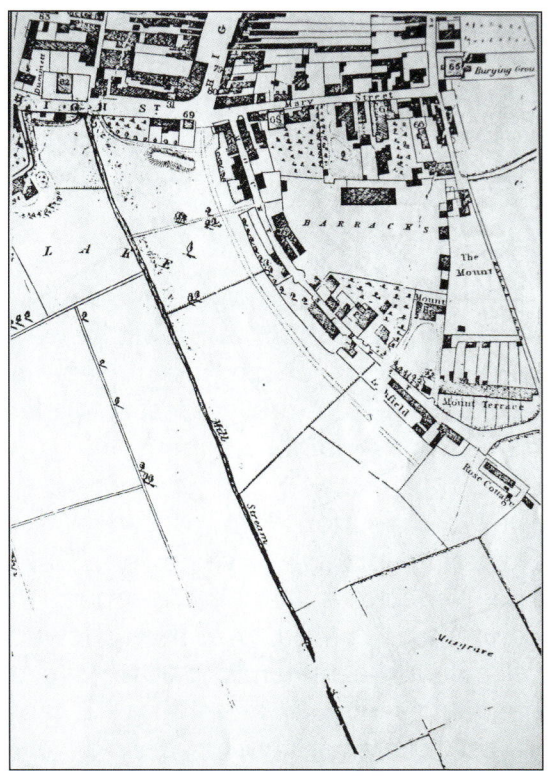

Wood's 1840 Map of Taunton showing Vivary Park edged by the stream and Mount Street.

Vivary Park as shown on Wood's 1840 map. The Park, as we know it today, did not exist. In its place were about five acres of fields or parkland, owned by Mr. Kinglake and scattered with sheep and cattle. He had bought Wilton House and the parkland from John Hammet in 1810. In the contract there was a clause stipulating *'that the use of the said land was for a meadow or ornamental pleasure grounds and no buildings, other than pleasure buildings, were to be erected on the site'.*

The entrance to the Park was, as it is now, at the top of High Street but there were no ornamental gates. The public were able to stroll through the fields and Mr Kinglake allowed the area to be used for public entertainment and cricket matches at times.

The fields shown on the left of the stream were eventually to be used for the Bowling Green and Golf Course.

There were no Park Gates, War Memorial, Fountain, Bandstand or flower borders. A few trees were dotted around mainly near the entrance.

The Band of the West Somerset Regiment of Yeomanry Cavalry who provided musical accompaniment to the Shows. Mr. Summerhayes is seated at the centre front.

On **18th June 1851**, a big marquee was erected to house the large and beautiful collection of plants, flowers and fruit. Summerhayes band provided musical entertainment. A beautiful bunch of wax flowers, displayed by Mrs. Melhuish, decorated the entrance to the marquee. Refreshments were provided at one end of the marquee by Mr. Wickenden who had decorated the area with a bunch of flowers made of sweetmeats.

Pelargonium bicolour Amazon introduced in 1871 by Mr. Samson of Houndstone, Yeovil.

The nurserymen of the surrounding area, amongst whom were Mr. Kelway, who had just set up his nursery in Langport in 1851, provided spectacular floral displays not for competition.

The competition groups were for Flowering plants, Cut Flowers, Fruit and Vegetables and were open to gentlemen. A Mr. J. W. Warren showed calceolarias, achimenes, balsam and a precious geranium measuring 12 feet in circumference though only a year old. Altogether he took 18 prizes in every category except fruit, evidently his gardener was not too good at fruit growing as he received no prizes in that category.

Norton Manor house and gardens, home of Mr. H. King Sturdee, President during 1921 and keen exhibitor.

The show opened at 1 p.m., the admission fee was 1s. (£4.37 in current money) and the princely sum of £16.00 (£1,400) was taken at the gate. In the evening, the gates were thrown open for persons wishing to see the exhibition without paying and great numbers attended.

The June show was so successful that in September **1851** a second show was held and a few ladies won prizes in each of the categories. Bear in mind that once again it was the gardeners who did the work. A large marquee, purchased by the Society for the purposes of this and future exhibitions, was situated near some fine old chestnut trees, and a smaller tent was provided for the collection of fruit.

The Society provided a silver cup, supplied by Mr. Abraham of Taunton, competed for by nurserymen (open to all England) for the best stand of dahlias, 24 dissimilar blooms, which was won by Mr. J. Keynes, nurseryman of Salisbury. Spectators were allowed to purchase plants from the nurserymen which did not meet with everybody's approval! The Somerset County Herald and Great Western Advertiser reported *"visitors were solicited to purchase 'any of these at sixpence' or 'those at a shilling'. The reporter felt that it defeated the object of the show in some measure; 'for what should be a public amusement obtained by public subscription becomes a nurseryman's shop'.*

A competition for Cottagers was included with 15 classes including the Neatest Cottage and best cultivated garden. I am unsure as to whether the inside or the outside of the cottage was judged!

As well as the Gentry and nurserymen entering the competitions some of the gentry attending the show consisted of the families of General Sir John Slade, R. M. King of Pyrland Hall, R. K. M King of Walford House, A. Adair of Heatherton Park, James Vibart of Chilliswood, Rev. Cecil Smith of Bishops Lydeard, Mrs. Williamson of Mount Nebo house, J. R. Allen of Lyngford House, Wm Norman of Courtlands and Captain Barbour of Wheatleigh Lodge.

Aeschyanthus splendidus raised by Luccombe Pince and Co. of Exeter.

Dahlia Rachel Rawlings introduced by Mr. J. Keynes Salisbury 1854.

1852 – In May the first show of the year was held in Vivary Park and despite the very cold spell of weather in the preceding seven or eight weeks, the display of plants and vegetables was greater than any seen at former Exhibitions and the quality could not have been better. Nurserymen exhibited some excellent plants but did not receive prizes; Mr. Macintyre, Taunton Nurseries, showed a magnificent collection of azaleas, with cinerarias and pelargoniums: Mr. Stephens, Tauntfield Nurseries, South Road, Taunton, showed a beautiful collection of calceolarias, cinerarias, pansies and verbenas with a monster broccoli and other vegetables; Mr. Lake of Bridgwater had a fine display of plants, fruits and vegetables and both Mr. Lendon of Wellington and Mr. Kelway of Langport exhibited a fine collection of fruits and vegetables.

Owing to the presence of the Bath and West Society who held their first Agricultural Show in Taunton in June 1852, concern was expressed as to whether the June Show would be successful but these fears proved groundless. A marquee 130 ft long was filled on one side with roses and also the new verbenas and petunias were shown. In the report of the third show held in September, 1852, the Somerset County Herald and Great Western Advertiser commented on the absence of the working classes, stating:-

'Perhaps it would be worth while for the committee to consider whether some arrangement could not, on future occasions, be made for their admission. Very few of this class can afford a shilling for a treat of this kind, but many would not mind a few pence'.

The newspaper suggested that other shows charged 3d after a specified hour. This would have the advantage of swelling the Society's coffers and enable the poorer classes to enjoy a treat from which they were otherwise excluded.

Sir John Ramsden M.P. for Taunton 1853 -1857.

The June 1853 flower show was unfortunately marred by the news of the extraordinary announcement that after the unblushing bribery proved before a Committee of the House of Commons, Parliament decided on allowing Sir John Ramsden to retain his seat.

Ladies and Gentleman at once retired from the showground and scarcely any respectable persons were afterwards seen in the town.

However the September show of fruit and vegetables, especially potatoes of which there were 50 dishes, was unprecedented in the Show's history and elicited general commendation.

After each show a dinner was held for members, judges and nurserymen.

Contrary to other shows, the nurserymen at the Taunton Flower Shows in **1851-1852** purely exhibited their plants, but in 1853 they began to compete against each other, the class being entititled 'Best collection of Stove, Greenhouse and miscellaneous plants'. As the years progressed so the number of classes open to nurserymen increased.

At the June **1853** show a new class appeared *'To be competed for by Ladies only'*. This was for a basket of cut flowers and the 1st prize was awarded to Mrs. Newbury.

The Society was growing from strength to strength and in **1854** two shows were once again held. On 21st and 22nd June, a two day show was held, combined with a Poultry Exhibition for which the Bristol and Exeter and South Devon Railway Companies conveyed all birds free of charge and issued return tickets on both days at single fares from, Bridgwater, Highbridge, Langport, Martock, Tiverton, Wellington, Weston-super-Mare and Yeovil. The grounds were opened to subscribers and the public at one o'clock on Wednesday and 11 o'clock on Thursday; refreshments were provided by Mr. Wickendon of North Street, and the Band of the West Somerset Regiment of Yeomanry Cavalry, led by Mr. Summerhayes, played a variety of popular tunes throughout the two days. The entire exhibition was said to be one of the most successful of its kind ever witnessed in the West of England.

On the Thursday evening, on the Parade there were balloon ascents and a brilliant firework display, paid for by public subscription, and the band continued playing there until ten o'clock to a large crowd.

Unfortunately during the first day two ladies had their pockets picked. The thieves in one instance coolly depositing the purse into the pocket of a respectable tradesman, after clearing it of its contents.

The Somerset County Herald concluded a very full report with *'It would be much more satisfactory for us and the committee, if the towns-people took a more lively interest in this society and suggested that if the tradesmen supported both by subscriptions and influence it would bring in the gentry from the surrounding areas which would have a beneficial effect on their trade'.*

Some of the local nurseries who exhibited were :-

Vincent Slade of Staplegrove Nursery, Wreaths, bouquets, zonal pelargoniums.
James McIntyre, Taunton Nurseries.
R. B Hawkes Park Street, Fruit and Rose Tree specialist.
Mr. Hockin of North Town Nurseries, nurseryman, seedsman and florist.
John Young, North Town.
Thomas Carter, Wilton.
C J Dyer, North Street.
George Phillips, Staplehay, and Cheddon Road Taunton, nursery seedsman and florist.
Charles Sweet, Bridge Street and North Town.
Hammond and Stevens, Tauntfield.
Mr. B. Nash, Wilton Nurseries.
Mr. Poynter, St.John's Church Nursery, seed merchant and nurseryman.

Tomatoes 1869.

Apple Annie Elizabeth 1868.

The second show of 1854 was held on Tuesday 12th September. This appears to have been extremely successful so it is puzzling that we can find no reference to any more shows until 1866. Possibly the fact that the Vivary Park Estate was advertised for sale on 27th September, 1854 may have had some bearing on the use of the Park. The auctioneer made the following comments:

'Lot No. 11 (being the Vivary Park) with its river boundary, would seem almost to force a claim on individual and public bodies taking an interest in social improvement, as an area fitted beyond every other in Taunton for one of those Ornamental Enclosures for rational recreation and resort now so frequently to be met with in other Towns, and where it has been deemed essential by such means to sustain and secure for themselves an influential inhabitancy'.

Vivary Park was sold but then purchased back by Dr. Kinglake, who then continued to allow it to be used for public access on a few occasions each year.

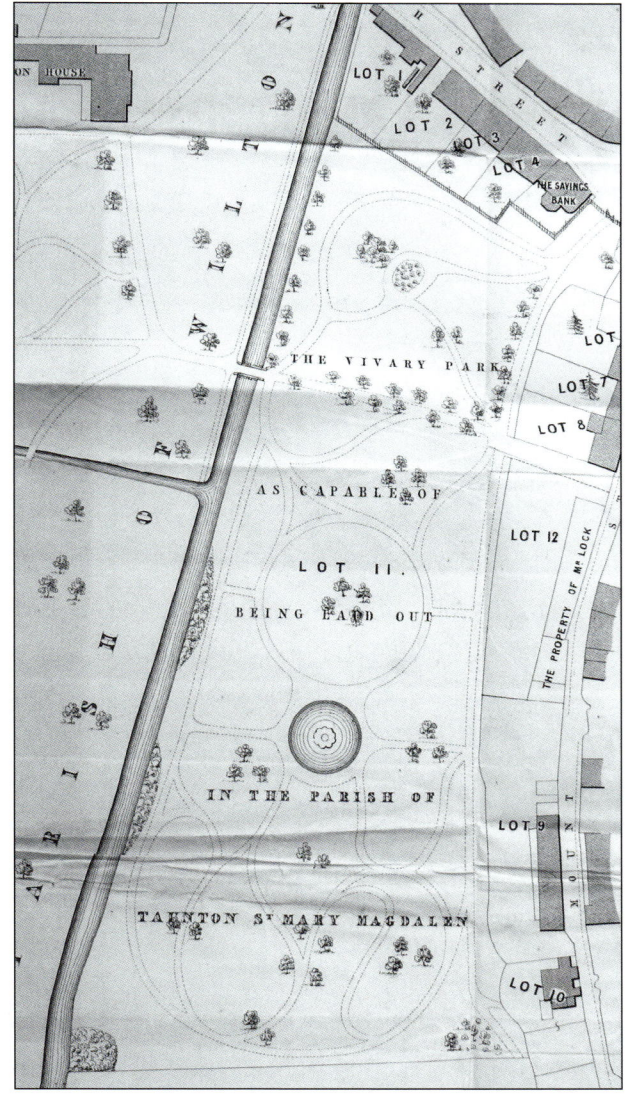

A plan of the proposed Park layout in 1854 when offered for sale by Mr. Kinglake.

Zygopetalum clayii.

Anemone japonica.

25

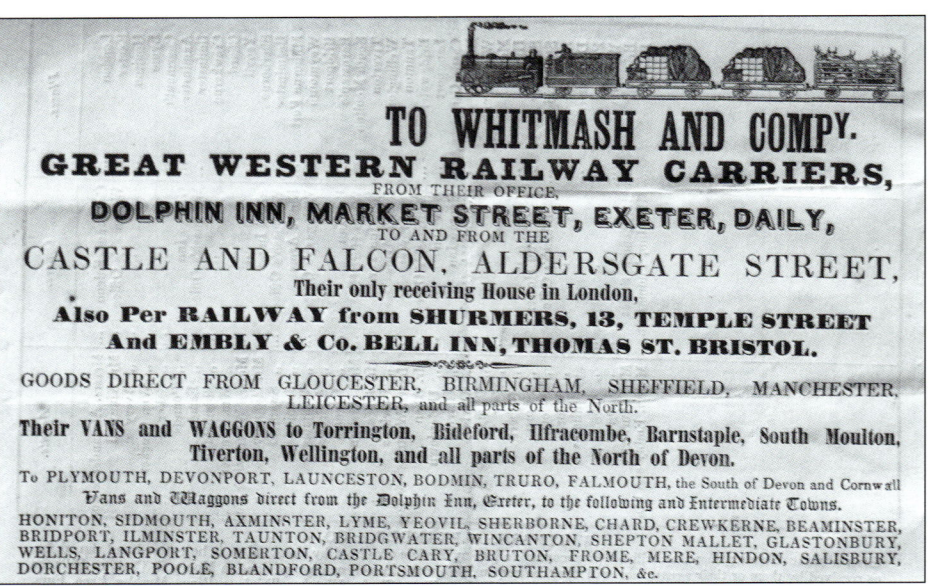

1840 Note the trains did not stop at Taunton but onward carriage was provided by vans and wagons.

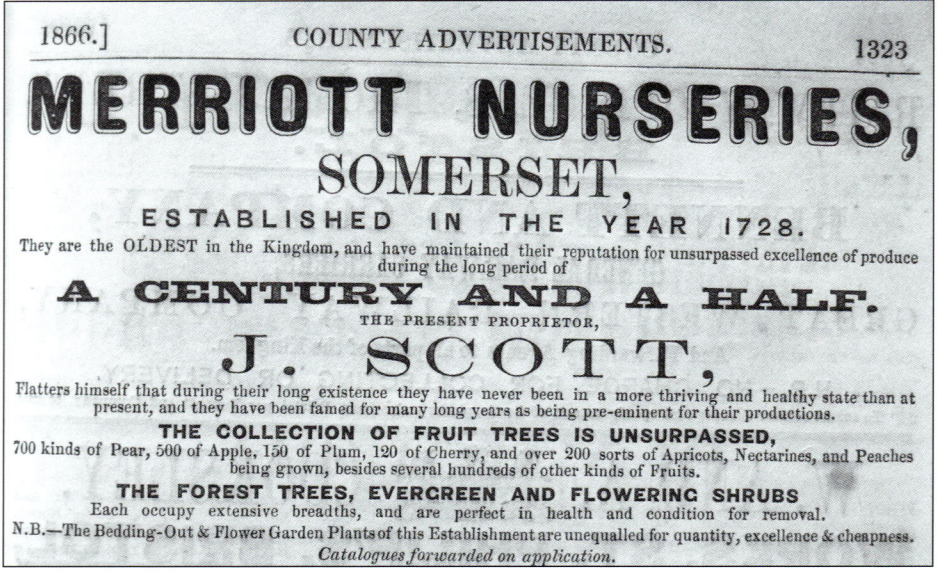

Scott's Nurseries exhibited at Taunton Flower Show and built the first outside show garden in 1924.

Advert from Veitch catalogue.

Stove and Greenhouse plants introduced in the 19th Century.

Cymbidium pendulum.

Banksia occidentalis.

Lelia perrini Veitchii.

Bilbergia moreliana.

Vriesia speciosa.

Tacsomia mollissima.

Cypripedium Harrisianum.

Cypripedium Lawenceanum.

Cypripedium Fairrieanum.

Another Beginning

In August **1866** the following advertisement appeared in the Somerset County Gazette.

> Vale of Taunton Deane Horticultural and Floricultural Society.
> UNDER DISTINGUISHED PATRONAGE.
> THE FIRST
> Grand Exhibition and Fete
> (*By the kind permission of Dr. Kinglake*)
> WILL BE HELD IN THE
> VIVARY PARK, TAUNTON,
> On THURSDAY, AUGUST 16TH,
> WHEN
> P R I Z E S
> VALUE
> One Hundred and Thirty Guineas
> *Will be offered for competition.*
> THE CELEBRATED
> Band of the Plymouth Royal Marines
> *Will perform on the occasion.*
> AN EXCURSION TRAIN will run from Exeter and intermediate Stations to Taunton, and Single Tickets for the to and fro journey will be issued at the Williton, Watchet, Stogumber, Crowcombe, Bishop's Lydeard, Durston, Yeovil, Langport, Martock, Bridgwater, Highbridge, Glastonbury, Wells, and Weston-super-Mare Stations.
> There will be a Grand Public Display of FIREWORKS on the Parade in the evening.
> J. B. SAUNDERS,} Hon. Secs.
> J. KINGSBURY,

The shows were generally one day shows commencing at 1 p.m. for members, the general public admitted at 3 p.m. and the Park being cleared of exhibits, tents and public by 6 p.m.

Later in the evening a firework display took place on the Parade, Taunton which was witnessed by thousands of people.

Nurserymen came from Bath, Bridgwater, Bristol, Exeter, Langport, London and Taunton to mount stupendous displays of their plants, not for competition. In this way they were able to display their produce to advantage and probably take orders for plants and seeds.

A triumphal arch of flowers designed by Edward Jeboult was created over the entrance leading to the Park from the High Street consisting of a monogram of the Society, the Town's Arms and the motto 'Tulia's jewels for joy and gladness' and 'Flowers are the stars of the earth'. On either side were a figure of Flora & Cerce with fruits and flowers and a sheaf of corn.

The Society had thirteen Patronesses including Lady Anna Gore Langton and Lady Acland Hood; five Presidents including the High Sheriff G. Troyte Bullock Esq., the Lord William Hay M.P., Sir Alexander Hood, Bart. M.P.; thirteen Vice Presidents one of whom was Sir P. P. F. P. Acland, Bart; 18 Committee members, one treasurer, and two secretaries. There were 78 exhibitors in three large marquees, two for stove and greenhouse plants and flowers and a third for fruit and vegetables and the prize money amounted to 130 guineas. Two tents were provided for the committee and refreshments.

A Mr. James Trundell exhibited in the grounds of the show, a very tasteful array of ornamental pottery for the garden and greenhouse. The first trade stand!

At this time the population of Taunton numbered some 15,000 but swelled for the day by excursion trains bringing in some thousands of people. £130 (£5,700) in admission was taken for the Show.

The town from North Street onwards was decorated with flags, bannerettes and some businesses had mounted floral displays. On the Parade a fountain was erected surrounded by a pond and fir trees.

The classes consisted of:-
Division 1   Plants & Flowers open to all,
Division 2   Amateurs and Ladies Classes:
Division 3   Fruit:
Division 4   Vegetables:
Division 5   Cottages:
Division 6   Market Gardens

DIVISION No. 3.

Fruits.

	PRIZES.		
	FIRST. £ s. d.	SECOND. £ s. d.	THIRD. £ s. d.
80—Collection of Fruit, 10 varieties, but not to contain more than 2 dishes of grapes of 3 bunches each, 1 pine apple, 1 melon, 1 dish each of peaches, nectarines, apricots, apples, pears, figs and plums, and 1 pound of cherries...	5 0 0	2 10 0	1 5 0

Exhibitors in this Class not to compete in 81 or 82.

| 81—Collection of Fruit, 8 varieties, but not to contain a pine apple, or more than 2 varieties of grapes, 1 black, 1 white, 3 bunches of each, 1 melon, and the other kinds same as in class 80 | 2 10 0 | 1 5 0 | 15 0 |
| 82—Collection of Fruit, 4 dishes, to include 1 dish of grapes (3 bunches), 1 dish each of peaches and nectarines, and 1 melon ... | 2 10 0 | 1 5 0 | 15 0 |

Classes 81 and 82 confined to Exhibitors residing in the County of Somerset only.

Off to Taunton Flower Show perhaps.

The show was welcomed by nurserymen who travelled from Somerset and Devon as well as other parts of the country to exhibit their plants. They also competed in the Open classes which were open to all and there was intense competition not only between the nurserymen but also the gentleman of the surrounding area who were only too pleased to be able to prove that their gardeners were every bit as good as the professionals. There were, however, separate classes open to Amateurs and Ladies.

 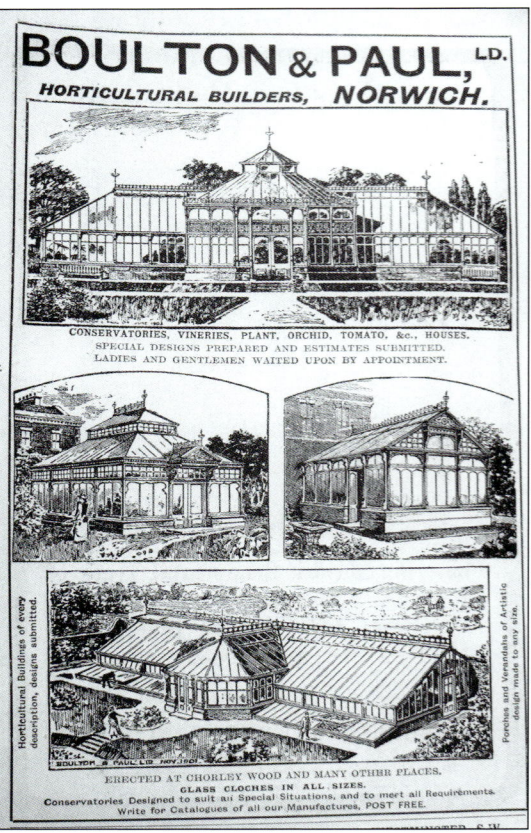

The sort of greenhouses available for the growing of plants both for Gentlemen and Nurserymen.

For the show in August **1867**, the bells of St. Mary's Church commenced ringing at 7 a.m. and, following the last year's success, the town really welcomed the Flower Show – floral decorations on both business and private premises commenced at the railway Station and continued up to Vivary Park. The town was 'en fete'.

The largest marquee, the Queen of the West, was 140 ft long, the Amateurs marquee was 120ft, the Ladies tent 90ft, and the Fruit & Vegetable tent and Cottagers tent were both 80ft long. There were a total of 111 exhibitors.

A dinner was held in the afternoon for the Committee, Judges and a few friends. At 5 p.m. the admission price was lowered and there was a crush. The crowds lingered on until the firework display on the Parade. The day finished with a ball held in the Assembly Rooms on the Parade.

In **1868** the Park was opened to the public for the first time that year in honour of the Flower Show and the music was provided by the full bands of the Royal Marines and of the Somerset V. R. corps. The band of the 26th (Bridgwater) Rifle Corps played music on the Parade during the day and in the evening in the Park where a balloon race took place before a spectacular firework display, provided by Professor Gyngell. The display was enjoyed by thousands of people and £64.00 was taken in entrance fees.

There is also mention of a Honey competition, two classes – 'The largest quantity of honey taken during the season from one swarm' won by Thomas Shattock and 'Best box or glass 1868' won by George Hake.

In **1869** heavily laden trains brought visitors from the principal stations on the Bristol and Exeter Railway, the company conveying them at low fares. Visitors also poured in from the surrounding district in every kind of vehicle and the show was considered to be one of the most important and prosperous of its kind in the provinces. The Committee of the Society, in an effort to encourage the people of Taunton to welcome the show, offered three prizes for decorations of the houses and streets, £2.10s; £1.10s. and £1. Nearly every house and shop on the main streets responded by suspending a flag or banner but in North and High Street, the route from the Railway Station to Vivary Park, the decorations were of an elaborate character with a total of four very large floral arches being erected across the streets. Hundreds of people could not enter the park in the afternoon because it was too crowded and it was nearly midnight before the park could be cleared of people.

W E & T. Cousins shop decorated for the Flower Show.

F. Adams, Fruiterer and Florist, shop decorated for the Flower Show.

There were 120 exhibitors competing in five groups of classes and four silver challenge cups were awarded by the Society. The prize money was increased to 120 guineas and several newly introduced plants from America, Brazil and other faraway places were exhibited.

No Show was held in **1870** because the Great Agricultural Show was held in June in Taunton in the Bishops Hull area and included its own Flower Show. The Show was an amalgamation of the Bath and West of England show and the Southern Counties Association show.

It is thought this arch was erected in the High Street in 1874 by Mr. Edward Jeboult.

There followed an extremely successful period when the town welcomed the Taunton Horticultural and Floriculture show each year with streets decorated from the Station to High Street and along to East Street. Shopkeepers dressed their windows reflecting the horticultural theme and in the initial years triumphal arches were erected along the streets, each vying with the other for the substantial prizes provided by the committee.

Nurserymen exhibiting at Taunton Flower Show have often used this venue for introducing new plants to the public and in 1869 Mr. Keynes of Salisbury introduced the following roses 'Madam Rothschild' 'Duc de Rohan', 'Monsier Woolfield', 'Baron Hausman', 'Madam Hausman', 'Marie Beauman', and 'Fisher Holmes'.

Rose Fisher Holmes. *Rose Marie Beauman.*

Introduced in 1869 at Taunton Flower Show by Mr. Keynes of Salisbury.

New classes were introduced - Class 15 'Newly introduced plant with ornamental foliage' and Class 16 'Newly introduced plant in Bloom'.

In **1871** 9,000 people bought train tickets from Bristol to Taunton and ticket booths were set up in High Street for people to purchase their tickets before entering Vivary Park. In all 4,850 people attended the Show and 6,500 people for the fireworks in the evening. Five marquees were erected, 150ft x 50ft, 140ft x 50ft. 130ft x 30ft and two 90ft x 20ft. Prizes were offered by the Society for the best arches erected in the town. The full band of the Coldstream Guards was engaged to provide the musical entertainment and Messrs. Brock and Co. provided the fireworks in the evening.

In **1872** Messrs Lewis and Cocks, grocers of Fore Street, agent for the patent Beehives of Messrs Neighbours and Sons, exhibited a variety of hives in full working order.

The **1873** show was so successful with 100 classes for the gentry and 20 for the cottagers that there was a proposition to move the Flower Show to the Flook House Estate for 1874 but this did not happen and the show has continued in Vivary Park ever since.

The band of Her Majesty's Royal Horse Guards (the Blues) performed an excellent programme of music from 2 o'clock until half past six on a specially constructed bandstand and again performed for the fireworks. A bazaar to raise money for the re-building of St. James' tower was held at the extreme end of the Park and at right angles to the tents. There was also a small collection of implements, displayed by Mr. R. Hellard, amongst which was a model of his originally-invented self-delivery reaper which he claimed to be the only one capable of sheathing and swarthing, two horses being able to cut ten acres in as many hours. The show was funded by donors and subscribers to the Society.

Nurserymen came from Bristol, Cheltenham, Exeter, London, and Oxford, to compete against the local nurserymen for the excellent prizes and their plants contributed to make Taunton the finest show in the West of England.

In **1874** the first paid Secretary to the show was appointed – Mr. T. J. Sheppard

Dipladenia urophylla and Lobelia densiflora.

Dipladenia urophylla was discovered by Thomas Lobb one of the plant hunters employed by Veitch.

Lobelia densiflora, discovered in 1846 in Brazil, is now known as Lobelia siphilitica.

Both were new plants and grown in a stove house.

Orchid Miltonia spectabilis was first exhibited at Taunton Flower Show in 1877 by Messrs. Luccombe, Pince & Co. of Exeter. The flowers can be up to 3" wide and 4" tall and the lips are most of the time very flat and showy.

The plant was originally imported from the rain forest of Brazil and it was difficult to bring into bloom, having to be grown in a stove house.

No flower show took place in **1875** due to the Royal Agricultural Show being held at Taunton in the Bishops Hull area.

In **1877** the Flower Show was welcomed so much by Taunton that business was suspended for the day and the town put on a holiday appearance. Police constables were on special duty near the entrance and in the 5 marquees to control the crowds. There were 120 competition classes, prize money amounted to £250 (£11,425.00) and several Silver challenge cups were awarded. It was announced that *'The Flower Show is not only for enjoyment and pleasure but for instruction, especially to the 'labouring classes'.*

In **1878** to celebrate the Flower Show, the Committee arranged for a grand concert the night before by the Band of the First Life Guards with a London vocalist, Miss Helen Horne providing an excellent vocal accompaniment. Two Venetian Masts were erected at the entrance to the Park, bearing flags and painted shields and surmounted by golden Fleur-de-lis. The Society's bandstand had been re-painted, decked with flags and painted escutcheons and surrounded by a thousand chairs for the accommodation of the visitors. On the Parade, various stalls had set up selling cakes, nuts and the Coffee Company, recently arrived in Taunton, set up under the archway of the Victoria Rooms, selling tea, coffee, lemonade and other non-intoxicating drinks.

1879 saw the first classes for Wild flowers and hedgerow ferns which were well supported. It was felt, however, that owing to a cottager entering grapes, peaches and nectarines in the Cottagers classes, it would be advisable to have some accredited persons to check the various cottagers gardens two or three days before the show to see what was actually growing in their gardens!

In **1880** at the August Flower Show the judges announced that only one other flower show in the whole country surpassed Taunton and that was Clay Cross in Derbyshire. Unfortunately, however, the show had made a loss and Dr. Kinglake had been unhappy for some years at having fireworks in the Park. Since it was the revenue from the fireworks which allowed the show to be held the question was raised of not having a show the following year.

The show was held in **1881** however, schools closed and work in the factories and workshops in the afternoon were almost entirely suspended and cheap bookings on the Great Western Railway meant that the town was thronged with people. Seven marquees were erected in the Park, and the Society erected their own bandstand in the centre of the Park for the band of the 23rd Royal Welsh Fusiliers and the fireworks were held once again.

In **1882** a meeting was called in May by the Society to discuss the complaint that *'Gardeners of this County were not being treated fairly as regards to the competition at the show'.* Classes were open to all competitors throughout the country and it was hoped that a group of classes could be solely for competition for the gardeners in Somerset. Subsequently the classes were changed:-

Division I   Open to all England,
Division II   Open to Amateurs only, Ladies Prizes
Division III Fruits,
Division IV   Vegetables, Open to all
Division V   Cottagers' (Persons growing vegetables for sale, or any jobbing gardener, not admitted as competitors) Wild Flowers and Honey

The Somerset County Bee Association requested the Society to be allowed to hold a Bee show in conjunction with the Annual Flower Show. This was agreed eventually and in 1886 two tents provided an exhibition of hives, bees and honey.

Throughout the rest of the 1880s the firework displays continued to support the Show which grew in importance in the country, attracting nurserymen and exhibitors from all over the country, including the Marquess of Bath, Earl of Cork, and the Earl of Radnor. One of the judges remarked that *'of all the shows he had been connected with he did not know one that was more purely horticultural, and one which existed more solely to promote the interest of horticulture, without outside inducements to attract the public'.*

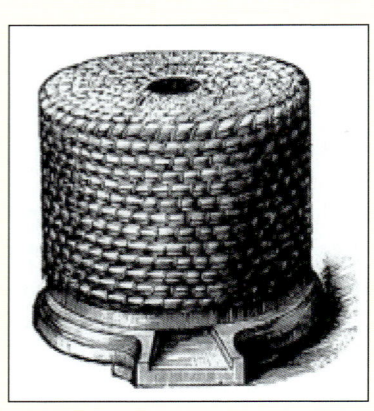

Skep or straw beehive 1880.

Pot Advert 1892.

The Flower Show became the most important social occasion of the year for the town and surrounding area. People came from far and wide with the railways offering excursion trains at reduced fares. People also came from the neighbouring villages in well-appointed brakes or even the humble donkey-cart. The shops and houses in the town always decorated their premises with flags, banners and displays for the day; people dressed in their best and the town was 'en fete' such was the importance of the show to the town, bringing in much business.

In **1889** the town council ordered that the street electric lights be left on all night to illuminate the town and the crush of people invading the town made it necessary to double the constables by bringing in reserve and country officers.

In **1890** the judges remarked that *'Manchester used to be the top show but now Taunton should be top in the country'*. Praise indeed.

Again in **1891** comments were made that the Flower Show that had just taken place at Taunton was the best in the West of England and one of the best in the whole of the kingdom in the present season of the year. The Flower Show coincided with a cricket match, champion county Surrey versus Somerset who administered Surrey's first defeat of the season by 130 runs, at the County Ground. 1050 people visited the electrical exhibition held in St.James Street which included a working potter, glass engraver and a glass blower all from London: The Poole Wall Manufacturing Company showed how collar stitching and button holing machines were electrically driven. However a comment from a Committee member remarked *'if it were not for the fireworks the (flower) show would run at a loss!'*

The Gardeners Magazine gave a Silver medal for an Exhibit of Exceptional Merit and in 1891 at Taunton, this was won by Dr. S P Budd of Barnstaple for Roses. In 1892 this was won by the Earl of Cork with an exhibit consisting of 10 dishes of luscious grapes, melon, peaches and golden plums in the fruit classes.

Military bands continued to be used to provide the musical entertainment both for the show and again for the fireworks in the evening. Subsequent Flower Shows were located on different parts of the Vivary Park, first near the main entrance from the High Street, then on the Ash Meadows side of the park, or alongside the stream. The show continued to grow and in 1898 in Division I there was a class for a 'display not exceeding 100ft'. Five entries were received and three had to be reduced to 50ft length through lack of space.

The evening entertainment in **1898** was provided by the bands of the Royal Artillery (Woolwich), 13th Somerset Light Infantry and the West Somerset Yeomanry who performed a descriptive drama to music entitled 'The British Army Quadrilles'. The idea was that of a night attack on an encampment and the various calls, parades and field exercise melodies were played. A volley of musketry and bomb explosions lent a tone to the mimic encounter and final victory signalled by the combined rendering of 'See the conquering hero comes'.

Throughout the years, on Show days especially, entertainment continued to be provided on the Parade by various entertainers taking advantage of the influx of people to the town for the Show. The town band was engaged by the Show committee to play, but also cake and toy stalls, usually doing a roaring trade, itinerant vendors of songs, glass cutters, patent corn eradicators, and *"the usual complement of minstrels and other street attractions"* were present. The streets leading from the station were also lined with fruit stalls, sweet stalls and shooting galleries in 1893.

The Town Council responded to the success of the Flower Shows by, in 1894, purchasing the first 5½ acres of land, from Mr. Kinglake, which would eventually form Vivary Park for £3,659 (£219,137.00) for the continued use of Pleasure Gardens.

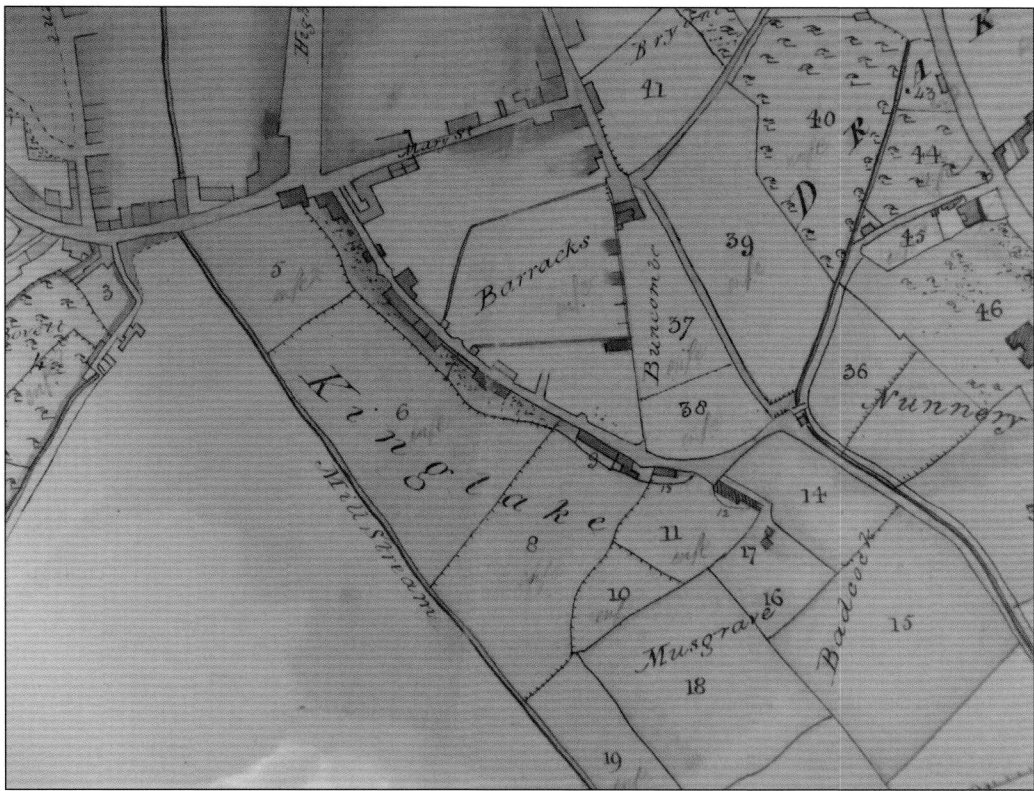

Map showing the extent of Dr. Kinglake's holdings Numbers 5, 6, 8 on the plan.

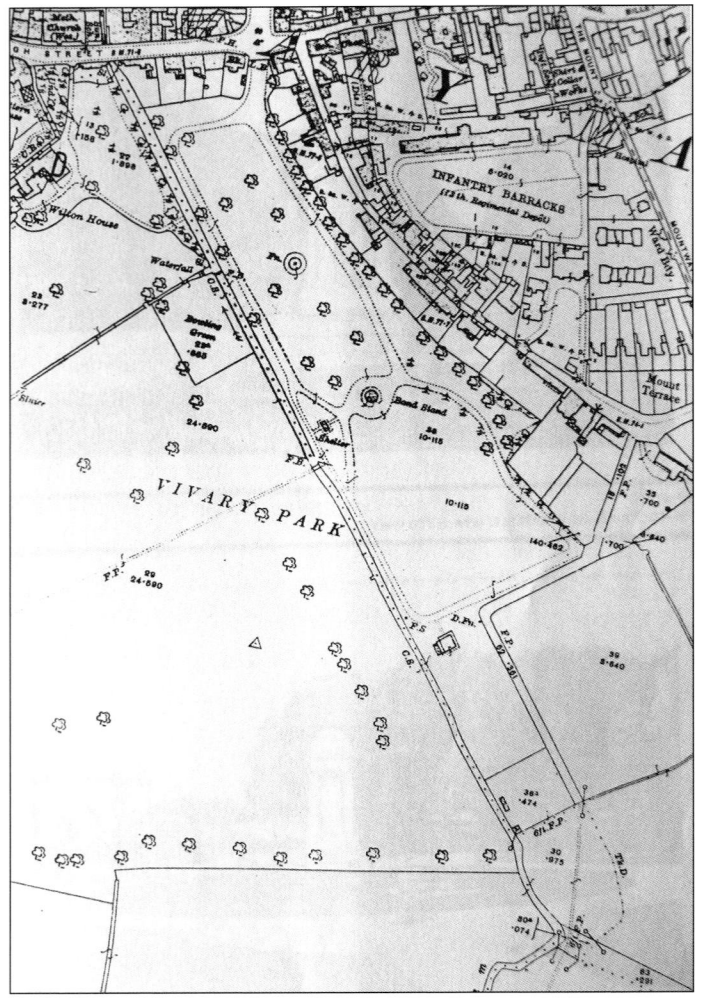

The town council also purchased extra lands from Mr Clatworthy and Mr. Fowler which included an established Tennis Ground, together with pavilion buildings.

In 1895 the layout of the park was designed by Mr. R. H. Poynter of Castle Green Nursery. The planting contract was awarded to Messrs. Veitch and Son of Exeter to provide 1,325 plants and shrubs at a cost of £128.10s.

The Ash Meadows end of Vivary Park with the Jellabad Barracks in the distance.

By **1902** seven exhibition tents were necessary to put on the Show, and a small fair of 'cheap jacks' was held on the Parade. Mr. Vincent Slade of Staplegrove Nursery displayed 70 varieties of pelargoniums and Veitch & Son, Royal Nurseries, Exeter included a new species of Kalanchoe Flammea from Somaliland, South Africa in their display.

1903 It was noted that other local shows had to have the services of a notary solicitor owing to disputes but the judging of Taunton Flower Show was so excellent that no complaint was ever laid. The judges were unqualified in their praise of the show and gave as their verdict *'that it was the finest in the West of England, one of the finest in United Kingdom and in some respects holding the first place in England, closely rivalled by Shrewsbury. Taunton had the finest show of greenhouse and stove plants in the country'.*

The Park Gates, Vivary Park installed in 1895.

The bandstand and shelter erected in the Park in 1895.

The War Memorial erected in 1922 commemorating the 1st Great War. Note the statue in the foreground, one of the seven statues donated to the Park by Mr. Alder of Belmont House, Haines Hill, Taunton.

Rose Dorothy Perkins.   *Rose Sunrise.*

Both roses exhibited as new varieties in 1904, together with Rose Liberty, by Mr. Vincent Slade, Staplegrove Nurseries Taunton.

	Exhibitors	Exhibits
1902	195	1,414
1903	228	1,530
1904	232	1,624
1905	228	1,628

	The Attendance	
	Flower Show	Fireworks
1903	4,178	7,225
1904	3,931	7,391
1905	4,555	7,403

A view of the Park after it had been laid out in 1904 with Jellabad Barracks in the distance.

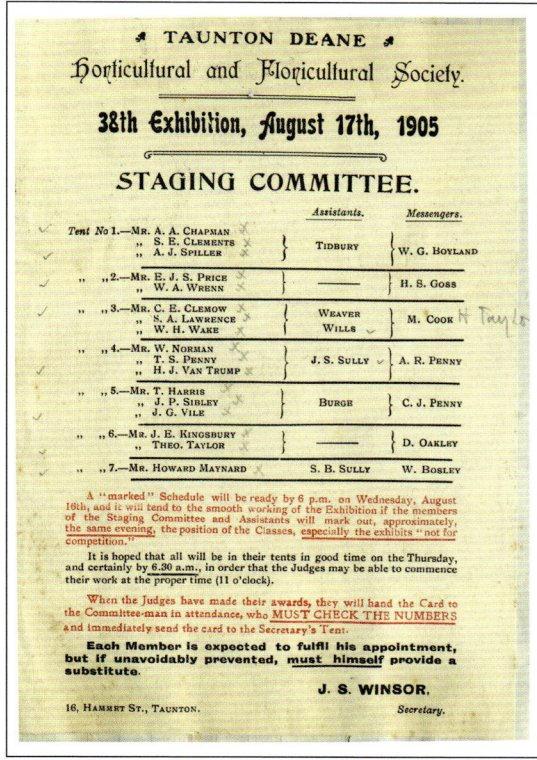

Staging Committee details.

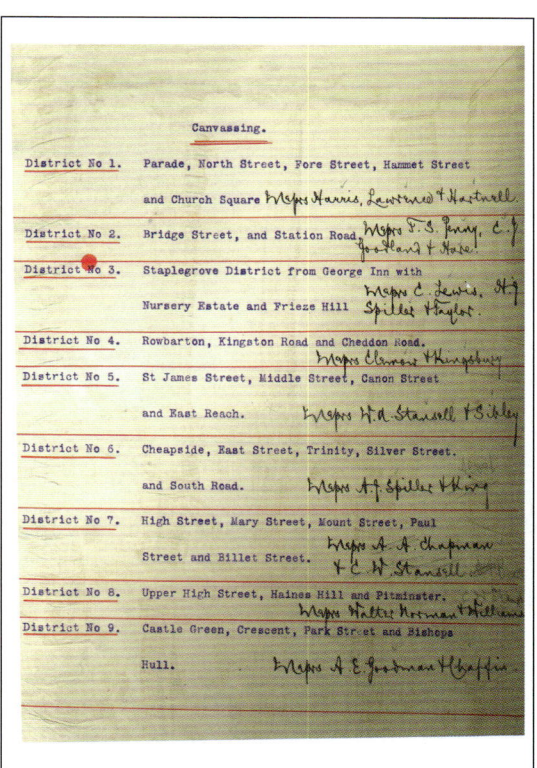

Canvassing district details.

1905 – By now a system of selling tickets had been developed with canvassing of the different districts of Taunton, volunteers who sold tickets from door to door. The idea was that no money would be taken on the gate, entry was by ticket only.

I draw your attention to the work of the Staging Committee. They had to start marking out the position of the classes from 6 p.m. Wednesday completed by 6.30 a.m. Thursday morning ready for the judging to commence at 11 a.m. The exhibits were staged between 6.30 a.m. and 11 a.m. Thursday morning. Once judging had been completed the Committee-man in attendance checked the numbers and immediately sent the card to the Secretary's tent for compiling the results.

1906 – the 1905 show was so successful that in 1906 it was held on the 15th and 16th August, the first two day show since 1854, and combined with the Taunton Fanciers Society (Poultry and Pigeon show) – newspaper headlines read *'Taunton Floral Fete;' 'Further High Praise from the Judges'; 'It has no rival'; 'Concerts and Fireworks in the Park'.* A new feature was a large tent devoted entirely to non-competitive exhibits, the forerunner of the Floral Marquee and the following year this tent measured 160ft long x 40ft wide, the largest marquee ever erected in Taunton. The marquees were supplied by Messrs W & A Chapman.

1907 – the Queen Victoria Memorial Fountain was erected and officially unveiled by the Mayor. With a gravel surround it had been placed unusually in the centre of the lawn to the north of the Bandstand with no paths leading to it.

The two day Flower Show this year incorporated a Forestry section in a separate marquee, the chief exhibitor being the Duke of Wellington of Stratfieldsaye, Berks. who provided exhibits of seeds, branches, cones and specimens of various trees. Lady Smyth of Ashton Court also contributed to the display as did the National Fruit and Cider Institute of Long Ashton, Sir Henry Hoare of Stourhead, Mr. Luttrell of Dunster Castle and other landowners in the area.

A total of five gold medals and eight silver medals were awarded for the first time in place of Certificates of Merit which had previously been given to the non-competitive exhibitors. A second tent was devoted to non-competitive exhibitors.

The Band of the Royal Marines performed at the Flower Show and finished each performance with God Save the King.

The Bandstand was erected in 1895 by the Town Council. It was supplied by Messrs H. Phillips & Son at a cost of £444 and was completed by 18th June 1895.

Previously for Band performances at the Flower Show, the Society had purchased a bandstand which was erected for each show.

It has always been a tradition of the show to engage a military band of repute to perform during the show.

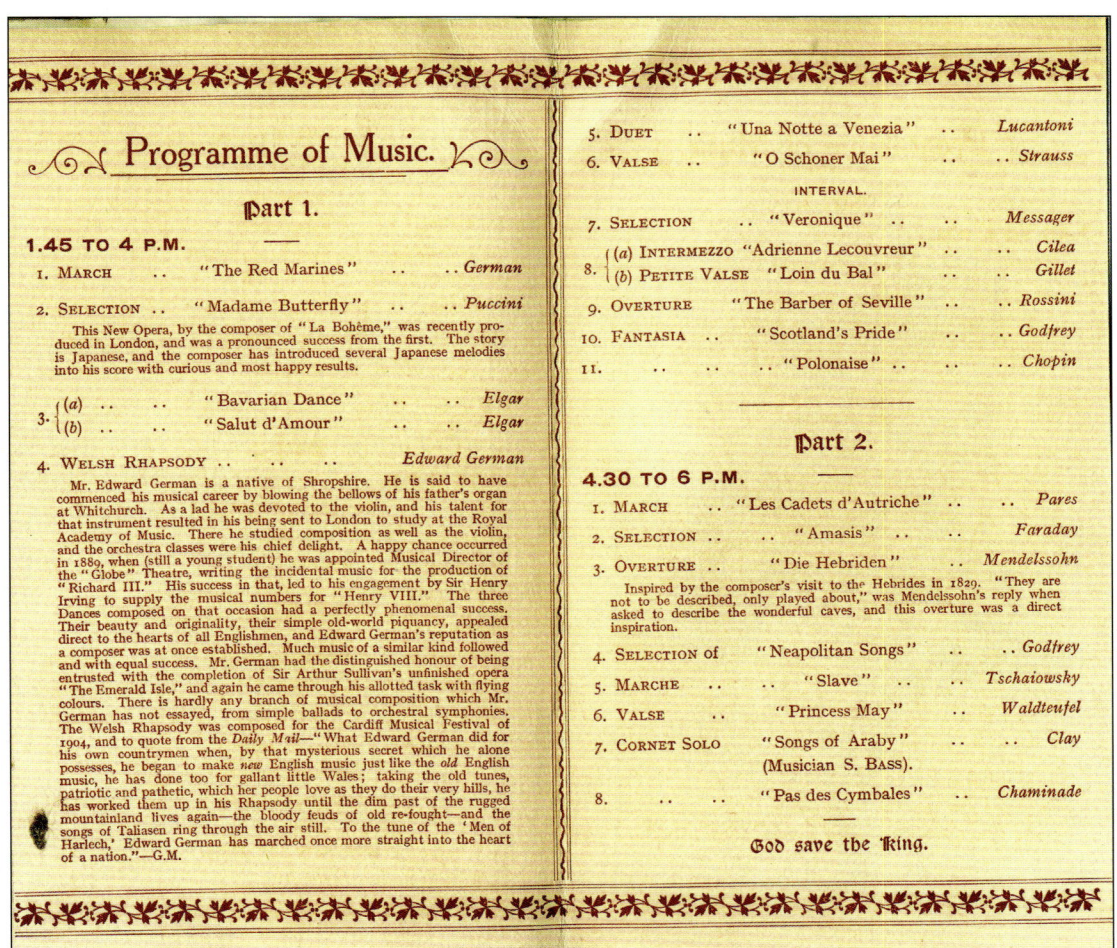

Part of the Band Programme for 1907.

1908 – Since the Flower Show had made a loss of £100 over the last two years the Committee requested that the Council allowed the Flower Show free use of the Park and the Council agreed to halve the charge of £10 10s.0d. It was suggested the Committee adopt the plan of Shrewsbury Flower Show by introducing various side shows to add to the attraction of the exhibition. Accordingly there were two performances of aerial acrobatics, on the Park lawns, at 2.30 p.m. and 6.45 p.m., after the Show had closed – possibly the forerunner of the Arena events in the present day show. The fireworks once again were in the Park at 9 p.m.

Side show attractions included:–
The Leros, funny eccentric boxers and laughter makers in their comic boxing act:
Mdle. Silvado, aerial gymnast, in her graceful performance on the aerial trapeze;
The Ladderites, in their wonderful performances on the aerial ladders;
The Seftons, grotesque comedians;
The Three Zaracs, comedy bar performers and a sketch "Mashing the Barmaid";
Don Pedro, the modern Blondin, in his performance on the high rope;
The Dunlops, comic knockabout bicycle and skating act.

In the evening Don Pedro went through his sensational performance surrounded with fireworks. Music was provided by the H. M. Scots Guards and on the evenings of each of the two days, they gave a promenade concert which on the Thursday evening accompanied the fireworks, the Park being lit by hundreds of electric fairy lamps as in previous years.

Gold, Silver and Silver gilt medals were awarded to the Trade entrants in the Non-Competitive tent.

Tillandsia lindenii var. Major exhibited by Mr. Williams of Victoria Nurseries, Upper Holloway London. He exhibited in the Trade Marquee at Taunton Flower Show from 1866-1880.

In **1909** a trade exhibit was staged by Mr. E. E. Chick of North Street, Taunton which featured garden furniture provided by the West Country Rustic Oak Company, Barnstaple. Mr. Chick exhibited various designs in seats, tables and flower stands, while a novel feature were the umbrella-shaped rose stands over which rambling roses could be trained. These contrivances would not only make gardens attractive but provide a means of shelter in inclement weather.

In the Forestry tent, as well as displays of tools, moths and butterflies, there were branches of trees showing various diseases. The Interior Department of the Government of Canada provided Canadian grown specimens of wheat, flax, oats and rye.

The Floral Marquee extended to 240ft this year, the largest ever erected, with 40 trade exhibits.

The King's Acre Nursery, Hereford took the Large Gold Medal and Certificate in 1909 for their display of fruit grown in pots. Amongst the display were fruit trees and vines six feet in height and bearing splendid fruit grown in nine inch pots.

The Competition Marquee showing Floral Art designs 1909.

Kelways advert.

Gladioli Ulysse, Raised by Mr. Kelway.

Despite the apparent success of the Flower Show it was felt to be declining so in **1910** it reverted to a one day show, opening at noon to the subscribers, with a new secretary and committee. The town responded by providing the biggest display of flags and bunting since the Coronation and the Committee arranged for the Territorial Band to play on the Parade from 10.30 a.m. to 12.30 p.m. There were no added entertainments at the Show but the Band of the Scots Guards played an excellent programme of music both in the afternoon and evening.

However, it was noted that attendance was not the same as in other years, possibly because there were other more numerous and varied attractions in the local area than previously. Cheap excursions to all parts of the country often drained the pockets of the working man and limited the support they could give to purely local events.

In **1911** an Elementary Schools Class was introduced for a collection of Wild Flowers collected in Somerset or Devon, fully labelled, in Division C Open to all school children. In the non-competitive marquee there were only 15 exhibitors as against 40 in 1909 which was a two day show. The nurserymen obviously felt it uneconomical to travel from Hereford, London, Oxford and Spalding for a one day show.

In **1912** gardening was being extensively taught in elemental schools in Somerset and the entries for the Elementary Schools Class increased - Braunton, North Devon, Castle Neroche, Corfe, and Norton Fitzwarren being some of the places the wild flowers were collected from. It was suggested that a shield could be provided for the winner and that the names of the schools should also be displayed on the prize cards.

Mr. Sholto Hare of Montebello, Weston-super-Mare provided a Silver Perpetual Cup for competition of Home-grown Fruit (Open to bona fide Amateurs only) This cup is still presented each year at Taunton Flower Show but now it is for the best exhibit of a vase of six border carnations.

1913 a special section of the Show was devoted to the Boy Scouts Association. Their own tent was filled with 202 exhibits of cut flowers, wild flowers, paintings, model garden furniture, pot plants, window boxes, hanging baskets, honey and photographs. 90 scouts competed for prizes and silver medals were given to the winning team.

One judge, Mr. Wm. Bates when interviewed remarked that he considered *'Taunton Show should be called the West of England Show as the displays were excellent, in particular Mr. Kelway's gladioli display which could not be bettered anywhere in the country and Mr. Cousins floral designs which were equal to anything shown in Regent Street, London'.*

The Bowling Green opened in 1907 alongside the stream at Vivary Park. The land was rented from Taunton Corporation.

In March **1914** the following letter appeared in the Somerset County Gazette.

This was the Committee's attempt to provide a fund to support the Flower Show, by increasing membership and to also ensure better public attendance at the show, thus, in turn, attracting more exhibitors.

However, the 1st World War started in late July 1914 and despite arrangements being well in hand, the Flower Show Committee felt it necessary to cancel the 13th August 1914 show and the letter shown below was sent to exhibitors.

In March **1915** the Committee met and it was unanimously resolved not to hold the show that year.

Owing to hostilities the next flower show Committee meeting was held in January 1919 and it was agreed to hold a Flower Show in Vivary Park on 14th August 1919.

Allotment holders were to be allowed to enter Division E with Cottagers provided they supplied a Certificate from the Secretary of their Association stating that,

'to the best of his knowledge, the articles to be shown were grown in Exhibitors' Allotments or Cottage Gardens and that intending exhibitors belong to the class of Competitors for which these prizes are given'.

TAUNTON FLORAL FETE.

To the Editor.

SIR,—It is doubtless well known that the financial position of this Society has given the Committee some anxiety of recent years. The annual expenditure necessitated by the show amounts to over £600, for which the Committee are responsible. Unfortunately there are, during the summer, other shows and attractions which have a considerable effect upon the attendance at this show. The annual fête of the Society has for *nearly fifty years* been the chief event in the borough, and has come to be recognised as one of the leading shows in the country, and the Committee will not allow it to be dropped until they have exhausted every means of keeping it going. It was therefore decided at the annual general meeting to inaugurate a guarantee fund, so that the Committee may feel justified in continuing the show in view of the fact that there is always the possibility of a wet day. It is suggested that the guarantors should be responsible up to a sum not exceeding £1 1s each, but guarantees for larger amounts will of course be welcomed. The Committee earnestly hope that the public of Taunton will generously respond to this appeal by filling up guarantee forms, which may be obtained at my office. I take the opportunity of saying that the famous band of the 2nd Life Guards has been engaged to play during the next show.—Yours truly,

R. A. GOODMAN,
Secretary.

3, Hammet-street, Taunton, February, 1914.

Taunton Deane Horticultural and Floricultural Society.

REGINALD A. GOODMAN, F.C.A.,
Secretary.
Telephone: Taunton 29.

3, Hammet Street,
Taunton.

5th August, 1914.

Dear Sir or Madam,

Owing to the serious position of affairs in the Country the Committee, at a Special Meeting held to-day, decided to ABANDON the holding of the Flower Show this year.

Considerable expense has already been incurred in Printing, Advertising and Postages, &c. (estimated at about £100), and the Committee have had under serious consideration the best means of meeting these liabilities. They have decided to ask Subscribers to contribute one half of their annual contributions, which they estimate will clear the amount incurred. They will esteem it a favour if Subscribers residing outside Taunton will kindly remit their contributions by post, and Members of the Committee will wait upon residents in the town in the usual way.

Unless Subscribers, who have already paid their Subscriptions, express within a week a contrary desire, one half of the amount so paid will be refunded.

If Exhibitors will please retain their Schedules it may be possible to utilise the same next year.

Yours faithfully,
R. A. GOODMAN,
Secretary.

1919 – despite the difficulties caused by the war - insufficient time since the release of men to restore the gardens and greenhouses to their old state of cultivation, it was decided to hold the show on Thursday 14th August. The weather was very good and although the show understandably did not compare with the pre-war show days a very good display was attained. The display of flowers, fruit and vegetables had not been equalled elsewhere that year and the cottagers and allotment holders division was in every respect a credit to the exhibitors. Many of the entries were equal to anything that could be obtained from a gentleman's garden.

It was suggested that a cup be awarded each year for the finest exhibits in the show, irrespective of class and description. Alderman Van Trump, the Mayor, who had only been absent from the Show for one show in 60 years, and that was for his wedding day 50 years ago, gave £5.5s. for the cup to be awarded at the next year's show. Mr. Wright, judge and Superintendent of the Royal Horticultural Gardens at Wisley commented *'that Taunton had made a better after-the-war start than many other shows that pre-war had ranked on a par with Taunton, but now those shows ranked far behind Taunton. The successful revival of the Taunton Show was to him all the more noteworthy because no valuable cups were offered as at some other shows, whilst the prize list was not so large, although very good for the size of Taunton'.*

Miss Sibly became the first woman member of the committee – if you remember women over the age of 30 attained the vote in 1918.

Free passes for the show were given to the Alms persons of the Town Charities, Children of St. Saviours Home in Park Street, the Workhouse and also the soldiers in the Military Hospital.

Evidently the show in 1920 had been successful as an Honorarium of £40 was awarded to the Secretary. Messrs Jarman & Co. of Chard provided "The Jarman Cup" value £5. 5s. 0d. for the Exhibitor gaining the greatest number of points in classes for Cottagers and Allotment Holders. If the Exhibit was grown from Jarman & Co.'s seeds and labelled with their labels, each prize to count 'One Point More.'

Unusually a very wet day graced the **1922** Jubilee Flower Show but special excursion trains charging a single fare for the return journey and late return buses to Bridgwater, North Petherton, Norton Fitzwarren, Staplehay, and Wellington, brought many people to the show. Six marquees were erected, the principal marquee being 220 ft. long and there were over 1000 entries.

In **1923** Mr. R J Case of Staplegrove Nurseries displayed 50 varieties of pelargoniums He had bred and named nine pelargoniums after Somerset cricketers and in 1928 he bred three new pelargoniums, Staplegrove Beauty, Staplegrove Pride and F. W. Penny.

In **1924** the show was held on Wednesday and Thursday of Bank Holiday week and opened at 1 p.m. for subscribers and tickets cost 5s. (£10.60) At 3.30 p.m. admission was 2s 6d, (£5.31) and at 7 p.m. – 9 p.m. admission was 1s. (£2.13). Thursday the show opened at 10 a.m admission 2s. From 1 – 5.30 p.m. admission was 1s. and admission at 7 p.m. for the band and fireworks was 1s. including tax. The decision to have a two day show was necessitated by the growing size of the show and the fact that the leading professional exhibitors were not satisfied with a one day event. There was a substantial increase in the number of trade exhibits which formed such a valuable section of the Show. Exhibitors came from Bath, Bridgwater, Bristol, Cheltenham, Dorset, Langport, London, Minehead, Surrey, Taunton and Westbury-on-Trym. Mr. Scott of Scott's Nurseries, Merriott built a show garden outside showing what could be done in a small space with perfectly hardy yet inexpensive plants.

In **1925** an added attraction was a Rural Industries exhibition, organised by Somerset County Council, where articles were supplied by local craftsmen such as basket work, Bridgwater tiles, ironwork, farm implements, engraving and hand weaving. The new Oxy-acetylene welding was shown by local smiths which allowed iron implements, which would otherwise have been scrapped, to be inexpensively welded. Several Women's Institutes (set up in 1915) sent specimens of members work including needlework, fur gloves and embroidery.

1927 saw the fourth annual British Gladiolus Society Exhibition combine with Taunton Flower Show. The Gladiolus show was housed in a marquee 260ft x 40ft and was the largest gladiolus show ever seen both in this country and the United States of America as it out vied the American Society's New York show. Exhibitors came from England, Wales, Holland, Germany and France. The Abol Trophy, a solid silver three piece tea service, was won by Mr. Clarke of Greenway Nurseries for the best exhibit demonstrating the advancement of the gladiolus as a decorative cut flower and occupied a space of 100 sq.ft. Kelway and Son of Langport were awarded the British Gladiolus Society's silver challenge cup for 24 distinct varieties introduced since 1923 not yet in commerce.

Attendance Record for two day show			Gate Receipts	
Date	Flower Show	Fireworks	Flower Show	Fireworks
1924	4,606	4,228	£307.00	£201.00
1925	5,463	5,664	£598 } Total of Flower Show	
1926	5,782	5,520	£628 } and Fireworks	

Mrs. Brown has kindly recorded her reminiscences in 2012 of the Flower Show for us.

Mr. & Mrs. Grant

I don't know that the following will be of any use to you but …..for what it's worth …….I am eighty five and have some, if loose connection with the show, for as long as I can recall, as does my eighty six year old sister who has helped me with this.

In, we believe, 1923, our father was fortunate enough to obtain a job as second gardener, at Staplegrove Manor, under Mr. Nation. (I believe four were employed then, later three). The Manor must have been into showing and in three years my father must have 'learnt the ropes' and continued to show when he became Head gardener, in 1926, on the death of Mr. Nation.

My sister adds here – she believes that Mr. Nation showed for many years. When he died, Mr. Turner suggested they should give up showing for Daddy's first years as Head then see how he felt about it. She believes he entered in year two but has no idea to what extent. She believes four gardeners were employed in Mr. Nation's day but we recall only three in Daddy's time.

We lived in a house provided, on the estate, and my sister and I attended the village school. We believe we were granted an afternoon's absence to attend the Taunton Flower Show. (Did it take place in term time in the 1930s?) Our Mother bought material, at 6d a yard, in the sale, at Brakes, in East Street, and made new dresses for us to wear to the show. We wore straw hats, with artificial flowers around the crown, and long silk socks. It was an occasion obviously! I recall the long walk to the park but my sister recalls me being taken in the push-chair, but there my earliest memory stops. Our Mother wore a new, long-sleeved, home-made dress, stockings, well polished shoes, a new straw hat (one every year) and gloves, and we believe we wore white cotton gloves too. (One dresses for Taunton Flower Show!) It was a very important occasion in our lives.

On the evening of Boxing Day, out came the new, blue Sutton's seed catalogue and Daddy completed the order form, after much deliberation, ready for Mr. C.A. Guy Turner, the owner of Staplegrove Manor, to view, because he paid the bill. Mr. Turner attended the show, taken in his chauffeur driven car. There he was shown around by his Head gardener, when he took pride/interest in what actually went on in his walled gardens, greenhouse and vinery. He had no idea that Daddy spent his life preparing for shows – Summer, Chrysanthemum and spring: it was Daddy's life! (In Summer, Mummy expected him home by 9.00 p.m. He started work at 7 a.m. but came home for breakfast, lunch and tea).

We watched the after Show fireworks from a bedroom at home, but just once, Daddy was persuaded to take us to the fenced off area of the Show ground so that we could see them all, not just the high ones. Crowded in the extreme, he said,

"Never again" and that was the only visit to Vivary Park for the fireworks!

Unless I have a vivid imagination, one year there was a Fair on what is now the members' car park. Noisy, expensive, rubbish, far below the standard for the Taunton Flower Show, was his verdict, but I guess he was extremely tired. He had slaved for days/weeks, and been up all night, so day one was time to relax at home I guess.

This annual competition seemed to be between three Head gardeners, Mr. Faul(Fawl?) from the Convent (in South Road?) Mr. M. Farley from Triscombe House, Mr. Grant from Staplegrove Manor and later Mr. Tuffin from Watts House, Bishops Lydeard.

I recall under-gardeners arriving for tea, at our house, as they stayed on that evening to help with the packing.

Packing preparation began days before and Mummy was involved as well. I recall two metal buckets scoured to brilliance. An enormous roll of plain paper brought from the Somerset County Gazette office, in Tangier, was brought out from the under-stairs cupboard and cut to size by Mummy for the base of each bucket. Then, in went a cheese plate, paper, cheese plate etc, the plates getting bigger to fit the buckets – Mummy's cherished Dinner Service, and a few extras; forty five one year. She was the one who padded the grape boards with cotton wool and covered them with the aforementioned paper. There were slots at the top for the carefully cut stems to hang through. (Think standing photograph frames) (Single and double).

"Don't touch. You will spoil the 'bloom' on the grapes!"

There were long, lidded boxes with packing in the base and rope handles. These held small fruit like peaches, nectarines, plums, apricots, melons, raspberries etc. No second, third or fourth gardener would dare to touch! My sister assures me that my memory is correct when I say forty five plates were needed.

A pantechnicon had been ordered, by Mummy, for six o'clock (p.m.) the day before the show. I recall that of a local furniture remover turning up, and Daddy was not pleased. Poor man had totally misunderstood the brief and brought a second rate vehicle – never again! Chapman's had the right vehicle and the right driver. They did the job for years afterwards. (Chapman's is now Debenham's and I doubt whether they offer the same) The loading was Daddy's job, and his alone. We all know now easy it is to knock off a begonia flower and pots of begonias, five feet tall, and a long way around, would make a 2011 winning exhibit look like a seedling. I recall fuchsias of equal size. Always, I was amazed as I watched Daddy taken an enormous pot of …….. and carry it so gently to its next site.

One year, I was tall enough to be asked to travel with the plants, standing up in the back of the pantechnicon, holding on to a bar in the side, to yell if the plants were being shaken too much! (Health and Safety!!)

"Hold that cane with your other hand" That was to keep the enormous begonia as still as possible whilst the driver was told, and did his best to comply (Daddy didn't drive).

"No more than 10 m.p.h. A whole season's work can be ruined on this journey!"

Chapman's pantechnicon probably used to transport Mr. Grant's plants to the flower show.

Here, my sister adds; on the return of the Show, after the Second World War, Daddy continued to show until Mr. and Mrs. Turner died in 1955. By that time, the two gardeners, who had been 'called up', did not return to gardening and Daddy was left with Frank (a somewhat disabled man). At this stage, the back of the 'van' guarding the plants etc. became her responsibility. She recalls being allowed to carry potted plants, such as ferns and fuchsias, and placing them in their respective classes. In those days there were several marquees, allocated to a) fruit b) plants etc. unlike the large exhibition marquee of today. She questions, was it three pots of ferns (various) likewise coleus? There were cut flowers in boxes ready to be displayed in green vases (In 2010 someone exhibited hydrangeas in green vases just like those we knew).

"Don't forget the can", a red 'Hawes' one, a watering can with a small, brass plaque and a brass 'rose'. That, and all the boxes, remained under the staging.

Daddy, "I think Sam's got the best red gooseberries this year but my green ones are twice the size of the others". He was at home having breakfast, to get dressed in his best, to return to Vivary Park.

"Pity about the apricots, not too good but the only ones there this time", and all the judging was going on in his mind.

A change of clothes, and back to Vivary Park to take around the boss when the Show opened. For Daddy there was a financial incentive as Mr. Turner paid for all seeds, greenhouse and vinery heating. i.e. a coal boiler stoked by Daddy, manure from the farm, sprays etc. etc. whilst Daddy paid the entry fees and the cost of the pantechnicon; and the prize money was the Head gardener's perk. (£45 one year, was a fortune to a man who was receiving £2.10s. a week pay) (That year the two children (us) were given £5 each to take to the Somerset and Wilts Savings Bank, next to Vivary Park gates, to invest, and Mummy received the rest. I guess she invested it in equal shares, in the same bank).

On collection night, all exhibits were taken back to Staplegrove Manor and Mr. and Mrs. Turner had all the first prize fruit on the dining table. I guess we sampled the third prize!

Of course World War Two put a stop to the Show and disturbed the long established history of it, and then came the demise of many Gentlemens' estates. We believe Mr. Turner died in 1956. Colonel Burlton could not afford to carry on Staplegrove Manor as he received it without the fortune that should have gone with it. Staplegrove Manor went to auction and was purchased by a local builder, Mr. Spear, and changed into five properties. The cow sheds and garages became houses. Daddy had bought the house in which they had lived since 1924.

On the sale of the estate, the showing naturally ended, but Daddy's interest in the Taunton Flower Show never ended. By then he was on the Committee and also a Judge of the Cottagers' classes. Not showing himself, he judged the professional classes too until 1969, the Summer before his death in early 1970.

Mr. Grant's three children.

But --------- we must have been about ten and eight when we entered the children's classes in 1935. Yes, we went off together, picking wild flowers for the class that I believe read 'twelve sorts/varieties named with common name, Latin name and natural order.' That required the purchase of a fabulous, second hand book. 'Illustrations of the British Flora' its date 1901. I have it still. If I remember rightly, there were pressed flowers too.

We learnt an enormous amount as a result. I recall catching the bus to Crowcombe, staying over night with my Aunt there and, alone, next day, walking along the main road between Crowcombe and Staplegrove, picking the wild flowers I wanted for the classes I had entered in the Taunton Flower Show. I guess I was about fifteen at the time. No, perhaps older – when did the Show reopen after the war?!

Mr. & Mrs. Withers

I remember Mrs. Withers and her fabulous table decorations. Through her I learnt what an epergne was! After that came Stella Reid with her Victorian table decorations. (Her husband's family kept Reed's florists shop in St.James' Street). She persuaded me, when older, to enter the novices' class table decoration. I had finished it, at about 2 a.m. when she came across to have a look and to ask a favour:
"I'm a cloth short" she said. "I know your Mum has got one that would be perfect. I don't suppose you would run home and get it for me?" So, I set off, on foot, through a silent High Street, along North Street, through Chip Lane, past Taunton School and Thone (the Prep.) and the Staplegrove Inn, through the Duck Pond field and along what is now named Manor Road, collected said table cloth from a silent house, and did the return journey. I saw, was greeted by, just one man on a bicycle! People went to bed then in order to get to work on time, and it was a disgrace to be 'on the dole'!

Fast forward, and in the 1960s my son took part. A comb case in felt comes to mind, which the President of the Gardeners Association bought off him at the end of the Show! He too did wild flowers. Then it was his sister's turn, but she was seven years his junior so he guided her into Flower Show classes.

Mr. Grant's two great grandchildren.

Now fast forward to the present, and my two grandchildren, now twelve and ten, have been taking part for years. In fact, in 2010, my grand daughter won a class that put her name on a Challenge Cup that bore her Mother's name so many years earlier. Of course, they have received their newsletter, in Cheltenham, and are likely to be taking part in 2012.

In my youth, we did not own a camera and, to date, cannot find any photographs in connection with the Taunton Flower Show from my Father's day. We seem to have photographs from the Spring Show and the Chrysanthemum Show but not from the one you require. (We haven't given up looking) Likewise, the silver engraved Challenge cups now owned by my sister and me – won three times in succession and kept. (I hope Mr. Turner bought them a new one each time) There is no longer a Spring Show in Taunton – is there? A small chrysanthemum show takes place, annually, in the Cheddon Fitzpaine Hall, in Rowford – the once Taunton Chrysanthemum Show – lack of funds prevents advertising – pity.

My sister adds, on returning to Somerset, after many years away, again she entered in the domestic and craft classes for several years, one being the year when Vivary Park became flooded overnight causing the exhibitors, who had staged their entries on the previous day, to be told there could be no judging or show so – 'please collect everything but you cannot park anywhere near the show ground and Wellington boots are necessary'. When they arrived at the Park, they could not believe their eyes.

"No wonder we needed Wellingtons" she said. She added that the people in charge, during that time, deserved to be congratulated on their efforts. Despite the fear that her craft work might be spoilt, as she knew it was on tables at the edge of the marquee, not a thing was harmed. It had all been moved to safety nearer the centre of the marquee, so it was a case of 'seek and ye shall find'. And she found it all, in perfect condition.

Unfortunately in **1928** the Society suffered a serious decline in entries chiefly due to the absence of exhibits from several leading professional and amateur growers and the disappointing season for horticulture. Mr. Cypher, nurseryman of Cheltenham, who had exhibited at Taunton Flower Show had died. He had staged his firm's big group displays, which usually won first prize, for nearly 50 years. Norton Manor, Watts House and Staplegrove Manor had not exhibited owing to their gardener's ill health and Colonel Napier-Clavering, ex President, was unable to exhibit as his gardener had died.

However, Mr. R J Case of Staplegrove Nursery exhibited an 1100 sq.ft. display as a corner of a picturesque garden through which ran a flag stone path leading to a drooping pool and rockery. The herbaceous border was beautifully set out with many of the newest specimens of phlox and a bank of hollyhocks. The chrysanthemum edged path gave a hint of approaching autumn and the gladioli in the foreground gave beautiful colour.

Primly Botanic Nurseries, Paignton displayed plants from around the world including an Aralia Elegantissima, an extremely rare plant at that time.

Phlox Sweet-heart.

Aralia Elegantissima now known as Schleffera.

1929 – The management of the show underwent a re-organisation – in place of a Committee of 40 members, an Executive committee of twelve members was appointed, with support from the General Committee. It was agreed to offer entertainment for exhibitors - £10 (£453) was alloted to provide refreshments for the principal exhibitors at a social evening on the first evening of the Show at which the Taunton and District Gardeners' association undertook to arrange a concert. This activity continued until 1932 when it was agreed to discontinue it but continue with the usual luncheon in the Park on the first day of the Show (for the Committee and judges).

Somerset Rural Community Council was given a space for a tent to exhibit a collection of rural industries. In addition to the provision of a Tent the Council paid the Society a fee in consideration of the space allotted. Possibly this is the start of charging for exhibitor space.

1930 was marked by the British Gladioli Society holding their International Exhibition at Taunton Flower Show bringing visitors from Australia, Tasmania, United States of America, Holland and Germany. A display, 40 feet by 25 feet, of nearly 200 varieties of gladioli was mounted by Kelways at the south end of the special marquee. They won the Gladiolus Society's large gold medal for non-competitive groups, two championship silver cups and the "Daily Mail" gold challenge vase.

Not to be outdone the following year, 1931, saw the first visit of the British Carnation Society which awarded the "Daily Mail" £100 gold cup for the best scented variety to Mr. T. Stevenson of Cotham Green Nurseries, Hillingdon, Middlesex for his six blooms of Carnation Jean Brydie.

A new 240 feet marquee was purchased by the Society.

ABOL PLANT BREEDING TROPHY.
Value 75 Guineas.

Mr. Kelway of Langport won the Abol Plant Breeding Trophy which had never been competed for at the Show. It was awarded *'for the exhibit of any one kind, race or strain of plant, flower, fruit or vegetable, which shows the greatest advancement in plant breeding since the war'.* The Abol Cup is regarded as the blue ribbon of Horticulture.

Messrs Kelway secured the award with their "Langprim" gladioli, raised since the war which represented the large flower varieties crossed with the small hooded primulinus species from East Africa.

The Vivary Park was closed to the general public for the Wednesday and Thursday of the Show. Unfortunately, according to the reports, despite the presence of an excellent Flower Show with the added attraction of the British Carnation Society, the fireworks and good weather, public attendance was down with resulting financial concerns.

1932 brought the National Dahlia Society with their annual show and exhibition to Taunton Flower Show with record trade entries in both quantity and quality. The largest marquee ever was erected, 300ft x 40ft for the non-competitive section with exhibitors from Bath, Bridgwater, Budleigh Salterton, Cardiff, Chard, Cheltenham, Colchester, Edinburgh, Exeter, Farringdon, Hillingdon, Langport, Merriott, Middlesex, Norwich, Nottingham, Oxford, Reading, Salisbury, Solihull, Southampton, Taunton, Totnes and Worcester.

A miniature national Rose Show was provided by five entries in the Open Division. Roses were mounted on staging the whole length of the marquee and the winning entry from Mr. C. Gregory of Chillwells, Notts, showing for the first time at Taunton, won the premier award with 2000 blooms consisting of nearly 50 varieties, including the new variety Mrs. Sam McCreedy.

Rose Mrs. Sam McCreedy.

Dahlia Cups and Medals.

In the Dahlia Society's Show Mr H. Clarke, of the Greenway Nurseries, Taunton took first for decorative groups, together with the Abol cup. Mr Wm. Yandell, of Maidenhead, was a good second. Gold medals for trade exhibits of dahlias went to Messrs Dobbie and Co., Edinburgh; Jarman and Co., Chard, Somerset; and H. Clarke, Taunton. Messrs Jarman and Co. also obtained the Abol challenge trophy, value 72 guineas, for plant breeding, this being awarded their cactus dahlia Vanity, raised from seedling by exhibitors and selected for trial at Wisley by the Dahlia Society last autumn. Vanity is a glowing pinky bloom of miniature size, very useful for decorative purposes.

The Abol trophy was awarded to Messrs. Jarman & Co. of Chard for the newly introduced Dahlia Vanity. The Mother Superior of Burnham convent exhibited approximately 100 dishes of vegetables of all kinds as a non-competitive entry but the judges still awarded her a Large Gold Medal. Unfortunately there were no entries in a new class 'Collections of flowering and foliage plants' requiring a display of 40 ft. This was because the country house owners had reduced staff and could not devote the time or expense to the necessary cultivation of the plants for exhibition.

The gardens of the Franciscan Convent, Taunton.
Many prizes were awarded for the produce from these gardens.

The Somerset Beekeepers' Western Division honey section had increased entries, 167 as against 125 the last year, and very keen competition.

The president of the National Dahlia Society Mr. J. T. West remarked that *'he had been judging at the Royal Horticultural Society's Show the day before and he congratulated Taunton on a wonderful show and considered it ranked third behind Chelsea and Southport'.*

Despite the quality of the Show, attendance was again dropping and the suggestion was made that perhaps this was due to no attractions/amusement as at Shrewsbury Flower Show. Therefore the fireworks were held in the Park and not in the adjoining field as in former years.

1933 – Mrs. Wimbush of Triscombe House, was appointed the first Lady President of the Society. The show moved to Thursday and Friday mainly to avoid clashing with Exford Horse Show on Wednesday. A Beauty Competition and Parade of six packs of Hounds were included as attractions to the show. However, the weather and the public did not comply and with heavy thunderstorms on the Friday, public attendance was still on the decline. This was thought in part due to the fact that there were many village flower shows in the district and several other attractions which drew people away from the Flower Show.

Messrs Hawkes and Sons, a long established Taunton firm, staged an attractive exhibition entitled 'Everything for the garden'. A grand selection of hand and motor lawnmowers and wheelbarrows of every description, including the latest rubber-tyred patterns was displayed. A real novelty was a basket on wheels that could be used by ladies for collecting weeds in the garden - a most useful invention. The same could be said of a new pattern of combined poultry house and run. Messrs Mettham and Lewis, Taunton sports outfitters and the Taunton Gas Company had displays and the Somerset Rural Community Council had a special tent with displays of wood carving, iron work, pottery and lead work.

1934 reverted to a one day show due to heavy financial losses in the past two years but despite the unfavourable weather the floral displays were once again excellent. There were trade displays by Taunton Borough Electrical Department, Taunton Gas Light and Coke Company, Messrs Hawkes and Sons Ltd. Summer houses, greenhouses and forcing frames were exhibited by Messrs F. Pratten and Co. Ltd. of Bath, Harry Hebditch Ltd. of Martock and W & A Edgell Ltd. Radstock.

Dunns Motors Ltd. of Taunton had arranged a display under canvas of 1934 models of 'Humber' and 'Hillman' cars but owing to certain regulations they were compelled to dismantle the exhibition after lunch.

Because of continuing disappointing public support it was suggested in 1935 that the Society needed to raise funds during the winter to keep the show going, because Show day, which had reverted again to one day in 1934 could not generate sufficient income.

In **1936** Constance Spry gave a lecture on floral decorations and this led to new classes in Floral decoration being created in 1937.

In **1937** Mr. Kingdom Ward, botanist, exhibited an unnamed Erigeron plant found in Tibet 5,000ft above sea level. Messrs Napier displayed 2,500 carnations amongst which were the new varieties Virginia, Laddie, Bonanza and Mrs. Henry Napier. Cottagers and Allotment holders had two new classes of Cut flowers and Plants added to Division E. Division F (vegetables Open to All) for market gardeners was added and Division G, 10 classes for Women's Institutes was also added. Strangely enough though, in 1939 the heading for Division G became 'Classes for Members of Women's Institutes who do not employ a whole-time Gardener.'

There was an increase in the number of trade stands which exhibited mainly around the bandstand, arena acts were engaged, and an Industrial Craft Exhibition took place.

In **1938** heavy rain fell on both days of the show and this led to a big decline in gate receipts. Mrs Withers was the oldest exhibitor, aged 77 and this was her 40th year of exhibiting. A new Class was introduced – 'Vase of garden Flowers for Girls under 16' unfortunately there were only two entries.

29

Offered by Councillor F. C. SPEAR,

A SILVER CHALLENGE CUP

(Value £5 5s. 0d.)

To the Exhibitor gaining the highest number of points in Division A.

Won 1937 by Messrs. Jarman & Co. and Messrs. Kelway & Son (equal).
Won 1938 by Messrs. Jarman & Co.

The Cup to become the property of any Competitor who wins it two years in succession or three times in all.

Offered by Alderman J. C. LANE,

A SILVER CHALLENGE CUP

(Value £5 5s. 0d.)

To the Exhibitor gaining the highest number of points in Division B.

Won 1936 by Mrs. Wimbush, M.S.H.   Won 1937 by Mr. W. R. Hewlett.
Won 1938 by Mrs. Wimbush, M.S.H.

The Cup to become the property of any Competitor who wins it two years in succession or three times in all.

Offered by Councillor W. BRAKE,

A SILVER CHALLENGE CUP

(Value £5 5s. 0d.)

To the Exhibitor gaining the highest number of points in Division B 1.

Won 1935 by Mr. F. W. Penny and Mr. S. Shattock (equal).
Won 1936 by Mr. S. Shattock.
Won 1937 by Mr. F. Leamon and Mr. S. Shattock (equal).
Won 1938 by Mr. F. Leamon and Mr. W. H. C. Pratt (equal).

The Cup to become the property of any Competitor who wins it two years in succession or three times in all.

Offered by Councillor C. H. GOODLAND (Mayor of Taunton),

A SILVER CHALLENGE CUP

(Value £5 5s. 0d.)

To the Exhibitor gaining the highest number of points in Division C
(Classes 66 to 73).

The Cup to become the property of any Competitor who wins it two years in succession or three times in all.

In **1939** the show moved to a Friday and Saturday and shown here are some of the Silver Challenge cups awarded for gaining the highest points in the relevant classes.

Also awarded was The Iles Cup for Division E, won outright by Mr. A E Searle; The Taunton Traders' Association Perpetual Challenge cup won by Messrs. J. Webber & Sons for the last six years and the H S Hare Cup for Carnations; Mr. F. Leamon won the W. Brake Silver Challenge cup outright in 1939.

Note: Challenge Cups became the property of the exhibitor winning it two years in succession or three times in all. Perpetual Cups were held for one year only.

Between 1935 and 1939 due to cost, the military bands were dispensed with and replaced by the Yeovil Town band, Dagenham Girls Pipe Band, and Thornelli and his Accordion band.

In **1939** The following arena acts were engaged:
Les Treborres – Comedy Ring and Aerial Bar performance
Style – Hoop Juggler
Olla Podrida & his Performing Collie dogs
Clown Bobbie & Evelyn – a unique Clown act introducing chair balancing.

Despite the unfavourable comments regarding the new entertainment of a Fun Fair, with 'The Moon Rocket' and a 'strip tease show' the 1939 Show did well, mainly due to the thousands of people who flocked to the Park on the Saturday, not only to view the Show but also to sample the delights of the Fun Fair and the attendance at the fireworks numbered 7,320. It was a well known fact that the Flower Show was not financially self-supporting, needing the Fireworks to bring in much needed revenue.

The total gate receipts for the Flower Show amounted to £408.9s. 6d. compared with £271. 5s. for the preceding year. The receipts for the fireworks display amounted to £180. 10s.

The Secretary, Mr. G. H. Summerhayes remarked *'I think we shall be well on the right side this year. There are not sufficient numbers, of course, attending the Flower Show itself, but the fun fair attracted a lot of people. The attendance at the fireworks display was very satisfactory, the number being 7,320. You have to go back 19 years to get a higher figure – 7,400'.*

However, once again War intervened and no shows took place until 1946.

H S Hare Cup 1932. *Taunton Perpetual Cup 1933.* *S D Farley Cup.*

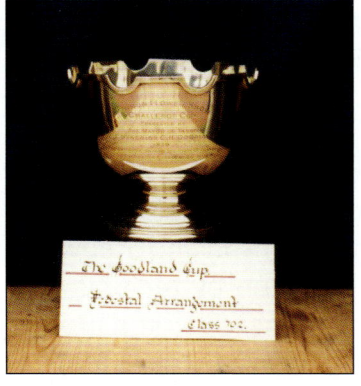

The H S Hare Cup was awarded for
1 vase of 6 Carnations.

The Taunton Perpetual Cup was awarded for
the most points awarded in classes 343 to 356.

The S D Farley Cup was awarded for
most points awarded in 225 to 259.

The Goodland Cup was awarded
for the floral art pedestal.

The Goodland Cup 1939.

1946 the Taunton Horticultural and Floricultural Society was able to hold a Flower Show once again in Vivary Park.

The Show took place on a Thursday afternoon and was part of the August Holiday Week. The Flower Show continued in conjunction with that week until 1953. (The Holidays at Home Scheme had been started by the Government in 1941 to encourage people to stay at home for their holiday week and featured dog shows, concerts, sports and entertainments in local parks countrywide). There were nearly 600 competition entries of a very high standard. Inside the tents it was necessary to marshal the public with the aid of the Police and a one-way traffic stream around the show tables. The attendance of 9,306 was a record.

The 2nd Battalion Gloucestershire Regiment entertained visitors during the show. In the evening 15,000 visitors assembled from 6 p.m. to 9 p.m. to await the fireworks.

1947 the Show had resumed two day opening not closing on the first day until 9.30 p.m, and it was so big in 1948 that it had to move to the adjoining field, now the Taunton Deane Cricket Ground, total floor space of the marquees being 26,000 square feet with 160 classes.

Taunton Industries Fair held in Vivary Park and the Taunton Flower Show held in Ash Meadows 1948. Note the very large Trade Marquee 440ft long running the whole length of Ash Meadows (top right).

1948 Messrs M & D Napier of Stepwater Nursery, Wilton who had begun exhibiting at Taunton Flower Show in 1946 exhibited a mass bank of 40 varieties of Carnations with three new varieties shown, Stepwater Coral, Stepwater Crimson and Stepwater Napier Supreme. The best display in the Trade Section was won by Mr. S. L. Best with a centrepiece of a Bristol bomber in statice and carnations, clustered around a harp in statice, carnations and sweet sultan, 'Gates of Heaven' in statice, dahlias and gladioli and a cushion of roses, lilies and cornflowers. He had only started his business eighteen months before.

There were 160 classes with 860 entries and the prize money and cups totalled £500.

1949 the now famous "Chelsea of the West" phrase in conjunction with Taunton Flower Show was coined once again when Judge Mr. W.. H Abbess, judging for the first time at Taunton remarked,

'I have toured the country and I hope you will consider it a tribute when I say that the Taunton Show could be called the Shrewsbury or Southport of the West. It certainly vies with those two big shows and even with Chelsea; Somerset should be proud of its exhibitors and its tradesmen'.

Once again the show was held in conjunction with the Industries Fair which was held in Vivary Park, the Flower Show located in Ash Meadows.

Kelway & Sons Gladioli display They exhibited at Taunton Flower Show from 1851 - 1980.

In **1950** the British Gladioli Society held their International Show in conjunction with the Flower Show and exhibits were flown in to London Airport from Ontario, Canada, Holland and the United States of America and brought down to Taunton by train. Two Dutch firms exhibited, each with 1,500 blooms, nearly all new varieties. However, Messrs Kelway of Langport were not to be outdone, exhibiting more than 2,000 blooms and capturing three Gladioli Society Championship awards, each of their trade stands won a large gold medal and they also had eleven first and three second prizes. Messrs. Napiers showed 5,000 carnations of 83 varieties.

By **1951** the Wild flower entries had grown so much that they were given a marquee to themselves. Classes for children under and over eleven had 137 entries and there were classes for adults also. The judges felt that the under-elevens showed outstanding artistic ability.

Judges said they felt that the great two day show, with more than 2,700 entries equalled anything they had seen in the country, even at Shreswbury. They praised especially the magnificent decorative displays, colourful trade stands and the wild flower section. The crowds agreed that the title 'The Chelsea of the West' was not an extravagant one.

In **1951** Messrs M & D Napier introduced another new Carnation, Taunton Flame on the 50ft x 15ft display of 5,000 carnation in 45 varieties.

In **1952** Messrs Napiers introduced the new carnation Lady Mayor in honour of Taunton's first woman Mayor – Councillor Miss M. A. Jenkin.

Scholars Encouraged

For the first time wild flowers had a marquee on their own. There were classes for children under and over eleven with no fewer than 137 entries, and also for adults. The judges considered that the under-elevens showed quite outstanding artistic ability.

The reason is that Mrs. F W. Penny (wife of Ald. F. W. Penny, chairman of the Society) and Mrs. W. Hart have for two or three years been encouraging Taunton scholars to see beauty in wild flowers and to cultivate the art of floral arrangements. This will surely benefit the show in the years to come.

Mrs. Penny told a *Somerset County Herald* reporter. "I want the scholars of Taunton to have a part in the flower show and to get to know and love flowers. On my visits to the schools this year I have been most impressed to find how flower-minded the schools are becoming. They are teaching children to love flowers, to choose colours carefully and to arrange them artistically. Schoolrooms are full of flowers these days.

"At 8.30 this morning the children competing were here in the tent arranging their flowers in vases.

"The way the adults are using wild flowers in their table decorations this year shows what can be done."

The committee had asked scholars to be careful in collecting their specimens and to avoid taking unnecessary flowers or otherwise damaging growing plants.

Mrs. Penny and Mrs. Hart are most grateful for the welcome they have received at the schools and for the teachers' co-operation. It has been most encouraging to find how many children, including boys, have exhibited.

The committee have also tried to give encouragement to young people by arranging a class for competitors under 18 in the decorative section and this has been well supported. The Society has sustained a great loss in the death of Sir Edward Anson who took a special interest in the decorative classes and gave a cup for novice competitors.

Report from the Somerset County Gazette of August, 1951.

In **1953** for the first time in it's 84 year history the National Rose Show combined with Taunton Flower Show, 40 rose growers coming from all over the country to compete. Taunton's great non-competitive marquee was 400ft x 40ft, 60ft longer than the year before, and was the chief attraction with two outstanding stands. Messrs Napiers displayed 6,250 carnations of 70 varieties, the biggest they had ever displayed. Blackmore and Langdon's colourful 50 foot stand of begonias which were claimed to be the finest in the world was deemed to be outstanding.

*Blackmore and Langdon's stand in the Trade Marquee.
They exhibited at Taunton Flower Show from 1951-2004.*

A new class was added 'Collection of vegetables open to village branches of Women's Institutes' for which a cup was offered by Mrs. L. R. Carter.

By **1954** the holiday weeks had ceased but the Flower Show drew even more people with a total of some 11,000 attending over the two days. The nine marquees occupied 76,000 sq.ft compared with 60,000 sq.ft. in 1953 which had also included the National Rose Show. Unfortunately the Show had lost £300 for each of the last five years and it was felt necessary to seek a wider range of attractions in association with the show.

In **1955**, when the Flower Show returned to Vivary Park, from its site in Ash Meadows, a Fun Fair was held from July 30th to August 6th. The Somerset Light Infantry band played martial music on the Parade on Thursday morning and in the afternoon and evening gave much-appreciated selections of light, musical comedy and orchestral music in the Park.

Once again the title 'The Chelsea of the West' was mentioned when the M.P. for Taunton Mr. Henry Hopkinson said *'One might say it is the Chelsea of the South West'.* 800ft of frontage was required to stage the non-competitive exhibits and there was a 46 class section for members of the National Association of Local Government officers with 166 entries.

Mr. F. W. Bond's colourful stand - he was an amateur who exhibited in the Trade Marquee in 1952 winning a Bronze medal for this display.

In **1956** the Fun Fair was sited on the Golf course, a bridge being laid to link the park with the course and a Gymkana was held in Wilton Lands on the Friday of the Show.

By **1958** comments were made that it was difficult to make any money, the running of the show had gone up 10 fold but admission had increased no more than twice. The secretary Mr. D A Smith pointed out that *'the Taunton exhibition is one of the very few national shows run on a purely voluntary basis and although Taunton Corporation have voted a guarantee of £200 it is only on condition that every endeavour is made to help ourselves'.*

Taunton Borough Council agreed that the Flower Show should have the sole use of Vivary Park on 7th and 8th August 1958 for the show and fireworks, the Convent field for car parking and Wilton Lands from 2nd – 9th August for the funfair. A new attraction was an exhibit from the Institute of Landscape Architects showing plans, sketches and photographs of good designs for small gardens. The Wellington Silver Band performed during the show and the Royal Electrical and Mechanical Engineers demonstrated their skill, including assembling a jeep in five minutes. The Army was also represented by the Somerset Light Infantry, the Royal Corps of Signals and the Royal Artillery. The show was moved to the South end of Vivary Park because there was no longer sufficient room at the north end. Luckily attendance was up, the weather obliged and the show was able to make a small profit.

In **1960** Taunton and District Winemakers Circle took part in the Show with 13 entries in four classes. Taunton Aquarists put on a display of tropical fish. A new trophy was presented, a silver spade mounted on a silver plinth for the best display of garden produce and won by Mr. C. H. Smith of Bishops Hull.

In **1961** heavy rain on the first day of the Show caused the postponement of the fireworks and a drop in attendance from 17,000 in 1960 to 15,000 despite an increase in exhibit entries. The show actually cost £3,000 to put on and the membership of the Society was still below 400. Each year different events took place in the show arena in an attempt to attract more visitors to the show. There were also a Careers and Craft Exhibition, a Go Kart demonstration at Wilton Lands, a Judo display and a trampoline display by Priory Boys School. The Junior Leaders Band from Norton Manor and the Taunton Town Band performed during the show. New competition classes were added – *'A Dinner table for a Golden Wedding celebration'* and a 6ft display of garden produce in the fruit section.

1964 – The Secretary wrote to the Taunton Corporation asking that they honour their guarantee against loss to the full extent of the loss i.e. £351.10s.10d. (£5,340) their guarantee was £400.00. The letter went on to say *'The Taunton Flower Show has a national reputation and may well be the only one of its kind in the Country, which is not financed by a municipal authority.'*

The Floral Art end of the Competition Marquee.

Two new cups were presented. The Hart Cup - a silver rose bowl for table decoration competed for by members of W.I.s and Townswomen's Guilds.

The Taunton Deane Cup for the best arrangement on a pedestal (Floral Art). This cup won outright by Mr. E. T. Dodd in the 1950's and was represented by him.

A new Home craft Section was instigated with 38 classes and this helped to swell the number of entries to 1,335 compared with 1,153 for 1963. The number of exhibitors also increased from 216 to 250. The show ground area was extended with a 400ft trade marquee inside which 25 of the country's leading growers staged a glorious profusion of flowers and foliage which included many of the latest hybrids and new specimens.

TAUNTON FLOWER SHOW
VIVARY PARK—AUG. 4th & 5th

"I have gathered here a posy of other men's flowers"

MONTAIGNE

After their disappointment last year when, for the first time in their long history, they were forced to ask Taunton Corporation to honour a guarantee against loss, the organisers of Taunton Flower Show are making an all-out effort to ensure the success of this year's show, which opens at Vivary Park next Wednesday.

★

Only the weather, which in the past has not treated the show too kindly, is left to chance. Everything else points to the show being a bumper success, with the exhibits and other attractions well up to the usual high standard.

★

From the inaugural show in 1866 to the present time, the organisers have been forced to struggle against weather adversities. No sooner were cash reserves built up than they were again reduced by a run of shows affected by rain.

★

In recent years the position became such that an appeal was made to the Town Council for a financial guarantee against loss and this was readily given.

★

At their annual meeting last Autumn, the Taunton Deane Horticultural and Floricultural Society, which promotes the show, announced that the total drop in "gate" money for the 1964 show was £299. The reserves were the lowest since 1939 and stood at only £562 in comparison with £2,500 in 1950.

It was suggested that the target figure for reserves should be £1,500.

★

At the same meeting an appeal was launched to increase membership and thus offset increased costs. Already the Society have been encouraged by the response to this appeal, and it is hoped that by this means a steady income can be achieved without being so heavily dependent on gate receipts.

★

The show, which is acknowledged to be one of the outstanding privately-sponsored events in the West of England, will again this year feature a number of attractions introduced at the last show.

★

The homecraft section, which last year added 38 new classes to the show, is being retained, with additional special classes for children, covering baking, knitting, sewing and embroidery.

★

Once again there will be well over 200 classes and the already impressive list of trophies contains the two new cups added last year. These are the Hart cup—a silver rose bowl—presented by Mr. W. Hart upon his resignation from the general committee of the Society and election as a vice-president, and the Taunton Deane cup, which was won outright by Mr. E. T. Dodd in the 1950's and re-presented by him for further competition.

★

The cups go respectively to the best group exhibit and table decoration by members of Women's Institutes and Townswomen's Guilds, and the best arrangement of flowers on a pedestal.

★

Because of the demand for space last year, the show ground area was extended, and this additional space is again being utilised. The tentage area will be as large as ever. Once again a special feature will be the trade tent, with its wealth of magnificent and colourful floral groupings staged by the leading professional growers.

★

In the competitive tent, it is anticipated that the number of entries and the standard of exhibits will be as high as usual, despite the difficult growing season.

★

There will be a galaxy of cut blooms, pot and foliage plants, delicious fruits and succulent vegetables to give pleasure to the eye—as well as, to educate, for there is much knowledge to be gained from a close study of the exhibits.

★

The decorative tent will provide much to admire in floral artistry, shades of colour, and original methods of display. The interest in this section has increased rapidly in recent years, and here again everyone can learn much by seeing how the experts add something to the natural beauty of flowers by their skilful arrangements.

★

As usual, the Society are hoping that the children's decorative classes will be well supported as it is from their interest that the Show will draw its strength in the future. There are numerous and varied classes for them to take part in, and garden produce and flowers may be used as well as wild flowers and berries.

★

The Society feels particularly keen that in these classes it is more important to take part than to win. The children will usually find a show judge or a member of the Society near at hand to talk over the exhibits, and one of the many pleasures of gardening is surely talking about it.

★

One thing that must not be left to be talked about until after the judging is the show schedule, which can be obtained from the show secretary, Mr. F. Pedlar, at St. Paul's House, Taunton. For the exhibitor a careful study of the schedule will avoid the disappointment of not entering exactly what is called for in a particular class. The schedule is also invaluable to the casual visitor so that he may more easily find the classes in which his special interest lies.

★

Besides the normal funfare there will be a number of interesting and traditional attractions.

★

Taunton and District Amateur Wine Makers' Circle will have ten classes in the open homemade wine competition which they are staging. Two challenge cups will be given for the wine of the Show and members of the Circle will also compete for the Percy Lock points cup.

★

Another interesting contribution will be made by the Taunton and District Division of the Somerset Beekeepers' Association, who will put on their annual honey show. The Association is offering over £40 in prize money, besides cups and other awards. In addition to the competitive classes there will be demonstrations of bees, honey and cookery.

★

Taunton Aquarists will again be showing the beauty of tropical and other rare fish. Another feature will be the exhibition staged by the Taunton Birdkeepers' Society.

★

The Taunton Town Band will be playing periodically throughout the show.

★

Special car parking facilities for visitors to the show are available (approach by Mount Street entrance).

★

In fact, this year, as always, the Society will be staging a show of which Taunton may justly be proud. There are few, if any, shows of its size run without the regular aid of public funds and it cannot be emphasised too strongly that the continued success of the show depends largely on local people giving Taunton Flower Show the support which it so richly deserves.

★

Make a particular note of the new show dates. The two days of the show are Wednesday and Thursday of next week instead of the usual Thursday and Friday show. This change was decided upon in view of the fact that the August Bank Holiday has been moved this year to the end of the month.

Chapmans have flowers in bloom at all seasons. In our Soft Furnishings Department they blossom on brocade and damask curtains, and on colourful loose covers. Dressmakers find them in our Fabrics Department — from the opulence of full-blown roses, to the neatest of daisy prints. Flowers prettily decorate the borders of pillowslips in the Linens Department, and are painted by hand on tea cups and plates in the China Department. On table mats and tea cloths, on hats and on handkerchiefs — flowers hold summer in memory all the year through. Come and choose some at Chapmans.

NORTH ST. TAUNTON PHONE 2626

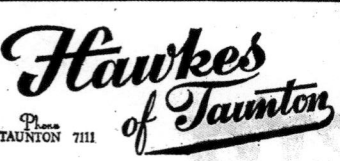

Phone TAUNTON 7111

FOR

EVERYTHING FOR THE GARDEN

SUTTON'S WORLD-FAMOUS **SEEDS**

FERTILISERS - PEAT - SPRAYS
TOOLS, etc.

A FULL RANGE OF MACHINES TO DO THE HARD WORK IN THE GARDEN WILL BE ON OUR STAND AT THE FLOWER SHOW

LOOK FOR 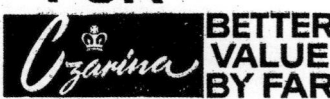 BETTER VALUE BY FAR

"CZARINA" is the special brand name given to a new increasing variety of goods, all of outstanding quality and value, created by the combined buying power of a national group of independent stores. Each item is thoroughly tested for quality and fully guaranteed—only at Clements & Brown in Taunton See "CZARINA" at the Flower Show—examples:

BLANKETS	BATHROOM SCALES
SHEETS	IRONING TABLES
PILLOWS	CARPET SWEEPERS
MEN'S SHIRTS	FAN HEATERS

+ + + SEE ALSO + + +

SPECIAL VALUE: FAMILY SIZE REFRIGERATOR, 4.6 cu. ft., three shelves big freezer, planned capacity door, table top; worth £47; fully guaranteed; free local delivery. Finest value obtainable at **32** gns., or 8 monthly payments of £4-7-6.

Clements & Brown
FORE STREET ★ TAUNTON 7777

JOHN SCOTT & CO.,
Merriott, Somerset
(2 miles North of Crewkerne, off A.30)
OUR ROSE FIELDS AND NURSERY ARE
OPEN
EVERY SUNDAY, 2-7 p.m.
ALL VISITORS WELCOME — TEAS AVAILABLE

DURSTON (Somerset) WOODLANDS

Rustic Garden Furniture
and Fencing Panels

Children's Play Unit

Container Grown Shrubs
and Ornamental Conifers

The advert for Taunton Flower Show 1965 from the 31st July, Somerset County Gazette.

In **1966** a Children's Corner was added near the boating pool with a model engineering display, radio controlled boats, pony rides, train rides and Coco the Clown. The proposed helicopter flights, landing on the cricket ground, had to be cancelled as the Ministry of Aviation refused to give permission. A demonstration of floral art and the art of Ikebana was provided by Shigeo Suga and Miss Soko Toyoshima of the Sogetsu School of Tokyo. The Japanese Embassy provided a special exhibit of flowers arranged in vases in Japanese fashion and the New Zealand High Commission provided an exhibit of plants peculiar to New Zealand. Plants were displayed from these two countries again in 1967.

Mr. Tommy Nash who exhibited at the Show for the first time in 1919. In 1966 he retained the Taunton Chamber of Commerce cup for most points in the Open Fruit Section. Here he is on the left of the picture with John Wyatt on the right, former floral art designer and whose family owned the Wilton Nursery, Taunton.

The British Pelargonium and Geranium Society and the National Sweet Pea Society put on special displays and the National Rose Society and the National Begonia Society each sponsored classes with the British Fuchsia Society awarding their special blue ribbon award.

In **1968** Taunton Parks Department entered a display in the Trade marquee for the first time, and won a large Gold medal.

Over the next few years the show continued to loose money, possibly because of bad weather on show days – nine shows in the last ten years had been affected by bad weather. In 1970 the layout of the show was altered – instead of hiring 5 x 40ft wide marquees as before, exhibits were housed in two 80ft wide marquees. The town council agreed to make a grant of £300 towards the show with a guarantee against loss of £100. The show lost £1,000 and in 1971 the organisers made savings by changing the catering arrangements and abandoning the official luncheon. The wine makers no longer had their own marquee but were in the Competitive marquee. The fireworks ceased in 1971 due to the steeply rising costs which no longer made it a sound financial proposition. In 1970 the fireworks had lost money and had to be subsidised.

In **1971** an innovation was the introduction of sales tables alongside the trade exhibits and nine exhibitors took advantage of this arrangement.

In **1975** amongst the displays in the Trade marquee were exhibits by Yeovil District Council, Tone Vale Hospital and Taunton Deane Parks Department. Taunton Deane's display featured a waterfall pool complete with pink and white water lilies and live goldfish against a background of blue convolvulus; Tone Vale Hospital displayed a fountain surrounded by perennial planting and the Yeovil District Council display featured a woodland scene. Denmans, the Taunton florist, provided an island display including about 30 different examples of the professional florists art from the cradle to the grave.

There were 43 traders, public authorities and voluntary organisations in the show ground and a one way traffic system was introduced, entry via the Mount and exit via Mount Street. This traffic system continued to be used until 2011.

The Flying Bugles Parachute team.

In **1977** the entertainment consisted of the Flying Bugles Parachute team from the Light Infantry Parachute Regiment jumping into the show ground on each day; the Royal Artillery Alanbrooke Band marched through the town from the Market to Vivary Park and then gave a marching display followed by a concert from the bandstand on the Wednesday; on Thursday the Junior Leaders' Regiment from Norton Manor Camp marched through the town to the Park and then performed for the delight of the crowd. The Committee doubled the prize money in the Trade marquee. Once again the traders put on an excellent show and this together with the entertainment gave the show a boost increasing the admittance to some 15,000 people.

Bonsai Display in the Trade Marquee.

Avon and Somerset Mounted Police.

1978 saw a record crowd of 16,000 attending the show over two days with a display by the Avon and Somerset Mounted Police, a power hang gliding display by Mr. John Long, Bands of the Royal Marines and the Junior Leaders Regiment. The numbers of outside traders were gradually increasing and Miss Julia Clements, one of the top international and national floral art judges said although she knew of the show's high reputation she was *'quite staggered by the quality and high standard attained'* that she described the show as "the Chelsea of the West." All prize cards were written out by Mr. Edgar Sweet, aged 70, who had been doing the job for over 40 years. Mr. Eric Rose, the Show Secretary, put the success of the show down to two factors *'The first is the very high standard we have always maintained in the displays, and secondly our programme of entertainment which I think is necessary if we are to attract the whole family.'*

1979 Disaster occurred on Tuesday 31st July when the competitors marquee was devastated by fire and £50,000 of damage occurred. The 280ft x 80ft marquee contained new trestle tables, paper, corrugated cardboard and floral art display backing but luckily no exhibits. The Flower Show volunteers swung into action - the Martock tent contractors were able to erect a slightly smaller marquee at 90 degrees to the old site, and several dozen volunteers reset the staging and 36 hours later the Show went ahead with a spectacular display of competitive entries.

A scene of devastation after the fire on Tuesday – arson was suspected.

There were now 250 classes competing for £1,500 in prize money. 16,500 people visited the show and the overall attendance, including subscribers, ticket holders and competitors amounted to 20,000. Coaches from far afield brought people to see the floral art displays. The Secretary, Mr. Eric Rose, expressed the Society's grateful thanks for the many donations, large and small, they had received from sympathetic supporters. New children's' classes were added and a Fine Art display was put on by local dealers. In the Craft Marquee, which had proved of particular interest in 1978, demand far exceeded the space available. There were a considerable number of applications for outside stands, late comers could not be accommodated as the showground was full with 60 outside traders.

Black Cats ladies motorcycle display team 1980.

Junior Leaders Regimental Band 1984.

The show continued throughout the 1980s with various band entertainments such as a West Indian Steel band, London Irish Girl Pipers, Esso steel band, the Moorfield Majorettes and the Dixieland Marching Band.

1982 A hot air balloon display and dressage displays by local riders, acrobats, an aerobic workout, the Mid-Wales Axe racing team, Moto Equestrians and Welsh Hawking displays all combined to entertain the public.

In **1982** a major row occurred – illegal traders were undercutting the prices of plants in the trade tent – exhibitors displayed stickers *'We are here under protest.'* Show regulations stated *'that nurserymen can only be allotted sales sites on the showground if they are prepared to provide acceptable displays in the trade tent.'*

Things appeared to settle down though for the following year. A few old faithfuls were missing but those who did attend provided some magnificent displays.

The Competition Marquee Gladioli Class.

By **1986** new classes were added, prize money increased and the number of Silver Trophies to be competed for was up to 28. The cost of putting on the show had increased to £28,000.

In **1988** there were 2,500 entries from 400 exhibitors.

The **1990s** were very successful for the show with the entertainment providing military bands, parachutists, a battle scene with descent from a helicopter and unarmed combat, Royal Air Force demonstration team of 16 men and their German Sheppard dogs, a gymastic team, musical rides by Avon and Somerset Police but more for the youngsters, gun dogs and falcons, dog display team, eagle and vulture displays, sheep dogs and an equestrian display by Olympic horsewoman Tanya Larrigan. The takings in 1999 were a record £30,000.

Mattock's Rose Display, they exhibited at Taunton Flower Show 1950 - 1990.

The Mayor and Mayoress of Taunton with Mr. Edward Du Cann M.P. for Taunton and Vic Verrier of Taunton Deane Parks Department.

By **1992** the cost of putting on the show was between £50 - £60,000 as against £28,000 in 1986.

In **1997** the Great Flood took Vivary Park back to its' roots. The Park stands on land that was formerly a medieval fish farm or *'Vivarium'*. Records of the 13th and 14th century show the Vivarium was in the ownership of the Bishops of Winchester and possibly covered 100 acres providing pike, bream, perch and eels for Taunton Priory and Taunton Castle and for the Bishop's household when King Henry III visited in 1239. The records show two ponds, the magnum vivarium, or great pond, which probably covered the present-day golf-course and the parvum vivarium or little pond, within which Vivary Park is situated.

Despite the heavy flooding and resultant difficulties in clearing the Vivary Park of all the exhibits, both competition and traders, the judging went ahead of what would have been a spectacular display of flowers in the trade marquee.

In **1998** the Flower Show committee agreed to wave entrance fees for traders who had been exhibiting at the 1997 show. With very fine weather the two day show was a success and the show president, Mr. David Nicholson, M.P. for Taunton, was moved to comment that *'despite suggestions the flower show should move to the foothills of the Blackdowns, it was very much a Taunton event, and any idea of leaving Vivary Park was now "dead and buried."'*

The Floral Marquee and a corner of the Competition Marquee 1997.

Between **2000 - 2004** despite spectacular displays and record entries in the Competition marquee, and record attendances, the Shows continued to make financial losses.

In **2005** changes were made to the Committee responsible for running the show and with the introduction and innovation of new ideas, the show began moving back to financial stability.

New attractions have included the Show Gardens, a class created for budding garden designers to create a garden in a small space; a Rural Crafts section featuring working displays; a Ready Steady Garden competition where a designer has a limited budget and time to build a small garden in just two hours; a dedicated Children's Area with separate entertainment; the return of the Taunton and District Wine Circle with various competition classes and an evening concert. With a move to Friday and Saturday the Show has continued to attract more visitors.

One of the outside Designer Gardens.

Outings for Members of Taunton Horticultural and Floricultural Society 2004-5.

The Titum Arum plant seen by members at Kew Gardens during their visit there in April 2005.

The Jade Plant Strongylodon macrobotrys seen by members at the Royal Horticultural Gardens Wisley during their visit in June 2005.

Members of Taunton Flower Show at Westombirt Arboretum in November 2004 on their inaugural coach trip, led by Vice President James Harris, third from right.

Chairman Lt. Col. Bob Homeshaw 2004 - *Para-Olympian Gold Medallist Debbie Criddle 2005.*

One of the many artistic displays mounted in the Floral Marquee.

Floral Art at it's best in the Competition Marquee.

*Three stalwart Vice Presidents at Work.
From left to right Les Richards, Peter Keirl and Mike Wilkins.*

A view of the Monkton Elm Garden Centre show garden 2012.

The re-named Floral Marquee, formerly the Trade Marquee, still mounts tremendous floral displays with traders coming from Bury St. Edmonds, Cheshire, Cornwall, Devon, Glamorgan, Hampshire, Norfolk, North Wales, Warwickshire, Worcestershire, Wiltshire as well as Somerset. Alongside the well supported Competitive Marquee and Beekeepers Marquee, there is also a flourishing Craft Marquee, Food Marquee, Rural Crafts area, a dedicated Children's' Area, Designer Gardens, Ready Steady Garden, many varied outside Trade stands and entertainment in the Arena. Something to appeal to all the family. But above all the Taunton Horticultural and Floricultural Society has remained true to its original stated aims that of:-

'the encouragement of horticulture in its various branches, by means of premiums to be given for the best specimens of flowers, fruit and vegetables to be exhibited at meetings held for the purpose and supported by small annual contributions.'

As a newspaper commented in 1854 -
"Altogether we are justified in pronouncing the exhibition to have been the most successful of it's kind ever witnessed in the West of England".

I think this is still true and we should all be very proud of Taunton Flower Show.

The author working in her nursery during her younger days.

Acknowledgements
I would like to thank my husband Robin for all his support and research into the history of Taunton Flower Show.

I would also like to thank the staff of the Somerset Heritage Center for assistance and guidance in our research, Nick Chipchase, Alain Lockyer, Somerset Archaeological Natural History Society and the Somerset County Gazette for allowing me to use their images.